The Daily Te

GUIDE TO
INVESTING

The Daily Telegraph

GUIDE TO

INVESTING

THE STRAIGHTFORWARD GUIDE THAT PROFESSIONAL INVESTORS DON'T WANT YOU TO HAVE

Rebecca Burn-Callander

Kogan Page

First published in Great Britain and the United States in 2017 by Kogan Page Limited

2nd Floor, 45 Gee Street	c/o Martin P Hill Consulting	4737/23 Ansari Road
London	122 W 27th St, 10th Floor	Daryaganj
EC1V 3RS	New York, NY 10001	New Delhi 110002
United Kingdom	USA	India

www.koganpage.com

© Rebecca Burn-Callander, 2017

The right of Rebecca Burn-Callander to be identified as the author of this work has been asserted by her in accordance with the Copyright, Designs and Patents Act 1988.

ISBN   978 0 7494 7793 6
E-ISBN   978 0 7494 7794 3

British Library Cataloguing-in-Publication Data

A CIP record for this book is available from the British Library.

Library of Congress Cataloging-in-Publication Control Number

2016037261

Typeset by SPi Global
Print production managed by Jellyfish
Printed and bound in Great Britain by Ashford Colour Press Ltd

*In memory of my daddy, who made and lost a fortune,
and whose advice would have been invaluable*

CONTENTS

ABOUT THE AUTHOR

Rebecca Burn-Callander is the former enterprise editor of the *Daily Telegraph* and *Sunday Telegraph*. A business and economics journalist, she has worked across national newspapers, magazines, TV and radio throughout the course of her career.

She started writing a decade ago as a junior reporter at *Real Business* magazine, before rising to become associate editor at the publication. She later became deputy editor of small-business website Smarta and web editor of *Management Today* magazine.

She specializes in writing about entrepreneurs and small businesses and has enjoyed the new challenge of dipping her toe in personal finance and unpicking the complexity of investing.

Rebecca was recently named one of the Smith & Williamson Power 100 for championing entrepreneurship in the UK.

She regularly appears on rankings of the best business journalists to follow on Twitter, where she tweets @sparky000 (a teenage handle that she refuses to let die). She is a frequent judge of business awards, a speaker at enterprise events up and down the country, and a driving force behind the *Telegraph*'s annual conference, The Festival of Business.

A Latin and English graduate from King's College London, she speaks Croatian, and has mastered at least five tricks with a hula hoop.

ACKNOWLEDGEMENTS

Many experts helped me to understand, distil and explain information on a wide range of investments. Special thanks go to Shaun Port, Alex Hunn, Lizzie Whitman, Andy Sweeney, Mohammad Kamal Syed, Nick Blake, Bob Dannhauser, Jonathan Hopper, Charlie Cox, Sarah Ryan, Rob Halliday Stein, Ed Maciorowski, Mark Blowers, Graham Wilson, James Adamson, Gil Hembree, Bruce Marchant, Roy Shaham, Rupert Patrick, Maria Jacquemai, Jaan Tallinn, Gwynne Dixon, Florian Leonhard, Charlie Burton, Thomas Schneider and the organizations Nutmeg, Vanguard, Coutts, Savills, Rapaport, Stanley Gibbons, Blowers, Crowdcube, and of course the *Daily Telegraph*.

For help in my hour of need, in a thousand ways, thanks to Neon Kelly, Rebecca Goodyear, Zoe Cormier, Vesela Burn-Callander, Flavia Fraser-Cannon, Elizabeth Anderson, Richard Dyson, Lily Silverton, Neil McNickle, Nataša Tomčić, Beatrice and Agnes von Kindt-Rohde, Daniel Slater, Emma Abson, Aurora Bellingham and Carl Reader.

Introduction

Terror. Confusion. Boredom. Anxiety. These are just a few of the emotions that the typical saver will feel when trying to work out the best ways to make a little more of their cash pile. For the amateur investor, the world of stocks and shares, commodities, and collecting for profit can seem impenetrable. Whom do you trust? Where do you start? Is there really such a thing as a safe bet in the fast-moving world of the money markets?

Whether you're a total beginner or a more experienced investor keen to learn about some new options, this easy-to-understand guide covers many of the various asset classes and alternative investments that are currently available to you. We will look at how they have performed historically and what the potential is for the future, get investing tips from the experts, and ultimately work out how best to protect and boost your investment.

This guide should give you a firm understanding of investment principles and explain many of the popular terms and phrases in plain English. This has two benefits: you will be able to understand the deals offered to you by financial advisers and investment experts – no one will be able to befuddle you with unfamiliar terms; and it should also empower you to make investment decisions on your own.

There is a myth that has been propagated by the City that so-called experts achieve much higher returns than the man on the street because they have the inside track, can spot bargains and have a sixth sense about when the market will turn. This is simply not the case. Nobody has a crystal ball, and recent studies have shown that 86% of fund managers have underperformed the market over the past decade. That means that most of the so-called superstar stock pickers underperformed the market. They still took home fat management fees, despite failing to generate the monster returns they promised investors. A typical investor would have been 1.44% better off each year if they had switched from an actively managed fund to a UK equity tracker, which is a passive investment that simply rides on the market's coat-tails.

Another myth is that you have to be fantastically wealthy to be an investor. There are a range of strategies available to people with as little as £5,000 to invest, going all the way up to £1 million or more. Don't panic if you have only a small pot to start with. You'll have to be more disciplined than an investor who can afford to lose more money than you, but that's a great way to learn.

The smaller your cash pile, the more attention you need to pay to the cost of investing. You may not be able to control the markets, but you can control this. Take the time to understand how much you're paying in fees for a financial product. Try to spot hidden charges. Cheaper doesn't always mean better, but the cost of the product itself can make a huge difference to your overall return.

There are many technical guides to investing available. These break down the maths of buying at one price and selling at another, providing equations that explain how much you make and lose if an index rises and falls. This is not a technical guide, and workings-out are only shown to make complex products seems less so.

Why do you want to become an investor?

Before we get started, you need to ask yourself a few questions. First, what do you want to do with your money? That's almost as important a question as where to put it. When it comes to investing, it can help to have an end goal in mind – even if it's just a figure.

Once you have your final number, you can work backwards and establish how much risk you want to take, how long you're prepared to wait, and bingo! There's your investment strategy. Do you want to buy a house, save for a child's university education, retire at 40, spend your twilight years as a beach bum in Thailand? Work out how much that will cost you, and that figure will inform your whole strategy.

Age is a factor here. If you're in your twenties, and are saving for retirement, you can afford to make long-term decisions and tie up some of your capital for many years. Later in life, you may want to dip in and out of your savings, or generate regular income to top up a pension.

Don't be fearful; don't be greedy

Having a magic number also guards against the twin demons that plague every investor: fear and greed. Both can cause intelligent, rational people to make poor decisions, whether it's getting out at the bottom of the market or piling in too much money at the top.

The really good investors sell when markets are rising. That's when there is real liquidity – people are piling in, desperate to share in the good fortune. By the time the wheel turns and prices are plunging, they're long gone. One piece of advice has come up again and again, from experienced traders who have seen it all. They say, 'Always leave some money on the table for the next person.' If you've made a tidy sum, get out and move on. There are more opportunities to be had. Hold on for too long, trying to maximize your return, and you may end up out of pocket when the market takes a sudden tumble.

Paying off debt > investing

The other question to ask is whether investing is really the best use for your money. If you've suddenly had a financial windfall, the best thing may be to pay off expensive debts. Store and credit cards, payday loans and unauthorized overdrafts can carry double-digit interest, and you'll make more cash, in the long term, by getting rid of those than you will in many savings products.

If you have a mortgage that you can pay off early, that may be the smartest thing to do with your money – unless there's a hefty penalty.

Paying off debts is far more straightforward than devising a brilliant investment strategy.

Depending on your profession, you may have the opportunity to do overtime, work extra shifts, freelance, or do bits and pieces of consulting. If you weigh up the expected value of these activities, and compare them to the value derived from spending that same time weighing up different investments, reading up on market movements or shuffling money from account to account, you may find that you'd be better off just working an extra few hours. This will only be true if your appetite for risk is quite low. Similarly, you could learn to spend less. Think of underspending like building up a muscle – you have to practise to get really good at it.

UK savers also now have the freedom to access their entire pension pots as a lump sum, rather than in annuities, once they reach retirement age, which is currently 55. This means that you can invest your nest egg to make more money, but you also have to remain aware that – if you lose it all – you don't have a lifetime to build it back up again.

Variety is the spice of life

The old saying, 'Don't put all your eggs in one basket', has never been truer than with investments. Whether you're investing £5,000 or £500,000, you want to aim to have a diversified portfolio so that if one investment goes wrong, the others can still generate results.

Diversification doesn't just mean many different investments; it means looking at totally disparate industries and asset classes. You want to have a good mix of equities, bonds and other financial instruments in your portfolio – and maybe even a few physical investments thrown in for good measure, such as gold.

Too often, people treat investing like a kind of lottery. They think they can just pick the right investment and get a big pay-off if they're right. But you may as well just go to the casino, head straight to the roulette table and put it all on red: it's the exact same thing. Good investors, the ones who consistently make money, take a much more cautious approach. They read the fine print, keep a keen eye on costs and don't try to pick winners – just have a good spread.

Some of the recommendations in this book require patience; the more reliable assets may take a few years to appreciate. That's the thing with safe havens – you risk less but the gains are more gradual. Never underestimate the power of compound interest, however. Albert Einstein is said to have called it 'man's greatest invention' – although this could be purely apocryphal. Imagine you started saving as a sprightly 22-year-old, and invested £1,000 at a 5% growth rate: that money will be worth £10,400 when you hit 70. Patience is key. If you cashed in at 42, it would only be worth £2,650.

The risk spectrum

There are scores of different investment opportunities out there. This book seeks to cover only the reliable, established, lucrative or up-and-coming options. These are arranged in an order that starts at safe – or as safe as it's possible to get – and ranges all the way to high risk. In the investment world, the higher the risk, the bigger the potential returns.

The average interest paid out by an Individual Savings Account (Isa), which is tax-free, is currently less than 1%, while National Savings & Investment's income bonds, which are 100% government backed, pay out 1% at the moment. The purpose of this book is to find asset classes and investment options that outperform these safe bets.

The idea is to ensure that beginners, who are just dipping their toe into the world of investing, first learn about the options least likely to lose money. Your risk appetite – the amount that you are prepared to lose in pursuit of gains – will become apparent as you progress through the book. By grouping investment options according to the likelihood they will produce a safer return, disparate investment options may end up sitting side by side.

What is a safe haven?

According to Investopedia – the online investor's dictionary – a safe haven is 'an investment that is expected to retain its value or even increase its value in times of market turbulence. Safe havens are sought after by investors to limit their exposure to losses in the event of market downturns'. Sounds wonderful, doesn't it? But safe havens change over time. The Swiss franc was viewed as one of the most reliable places to put your money until 2015, when several moves by the Swiss national bank created massive volatility in the market. Payday lenders and 'cash for gold' companies surge during a downturn but can be wiped out in times of plenty, when bank loans are easy to come by and wages rise.

The safe havens referenced in this book were correct at time of writing, but markets can move quickly. It's worth looking into the current state of play, and there will be signposts throughout the book to show you how.

To stay on top of market movements that may affect your investments, set up Google Alerts around your interests. Social media is becoming an increasingly valuable way to find out news about popular investables – many of the Twitter apps, such as Tweetdeck, will let you save searches so that you can see all mentions of a certain word or phrase easily. But be careful whom you follow. The internet is full of self-styled experts who have an agenda – usually to charge you for their expertise.

All the information contained in this book is intended as a guide, not investment advice. Any investments you make are undertaken at your own risk, and their value may go down as well as up. Never bet the farm.

It's also well worth your while to read up on the Financial Services Compensation Scheme. This is an initiative that kicks in as a last resort if you are left out of pocket by an investment business, or if you are given bad advice. It can pay out a maximum of £75,000 per person, per firm. But it only protects the customers of certain authorized organizations. They must be regulated by the Financial Conduct Authority and the Prudential Regulation Authority. You should always check whether your investment is covered before signing on the dotted line: there's an up-to-date list on the Financial Services Compensation Scheme (FSCS) website (fscs.org.uk).

Collectables vs investables – and why you should care

There is a lot of debate about the difference between something that is collectable and makes a good investment, and something that holds primarily nostalgic value, so this is a note on how we've separated the two.

A good friend of mine collects My Little Ponies from the 1980s. She loves them because they remind her of her childhood, their strawberry-scented manes taking her back to her halcyon days. She scours eBay for these toys and is happy to pay up to £30 for one that's in decent condition. These My Little Ponies are collected for her enjoyment. She doesn't want to sell them on later; she will probably give them to her children to play with one day.

Collectables are very different from investables. One must not get too emotionally attached to investables; they are acquired as a means of making more money, not as family heirlooms. They must be left untouched, stored carefully, and certainly never removed from their packaging.

The basics of investing dictate that you buy things when they are cheap and sell when they are valuable. Never forget this when buying items that are collectable.

If you feel compelled to buy something, at an inflated price, just because you loved the movie it refers to, or you had the same toy when you were five years old, that is not an investable; it's a collectable. Beware.

Remember, too, the theory of the 'time value' of money. This is the concept that money now is worth more than money in the future, based on the principle that it could be earning interest – even if that's just 1% interest in a savings account. If you lock up today's money in an investment that does not appreciate, you are losing out on that value.

If you're tempted by collectables – as opposed to the investables we'll be focusing on in this book – and have a wealth of knowledge about the items you want to collect, the expert advice is to become a dealer. Create your own network of buyers and scout routes to finding the collectables – never pay more than 20–50% of the retail value for the item. This is the only sure-fire way to make money on collectables where the demand for the items is relatively low.

Passion can make you a better investor

Many toy investors may choose to start collecting a particular kind of toy – Barbie dolls, for example, or LEGO® – because they remember loving them when they were young, and there is value in that. If you're going to spend a fair proportion of your time investing in a particular thing, it can help to understand and enjoy that product. Many of the investment options referenced in this book are in markets that are evolving constantly, and it's important to stay on top of new trends, and for that process to be a pleasure, not a chore.

But the investor must never lose sight of the ultimate objective: to achieve a return on the initial investment. Never forget that with collectables, especially new ones, you are ultimately buying the item at the retail price – unless you're a dealer – but may receive the wholesale price when you sell. There can be a substantial difference between the two, which destroys any appreciation in value instantly.

There are many interesting theories about the psychology of collecting physical items, and why certain people prefer this method of investment to trading intangibles such as stocks and shares. Cautious investors may feel safer knowing that alongside investments that happen purely on a screen, there's a physical object that they can attach value to. A digital number can easily go from 100 to 0, but a physical asset can't just be vaporized.

The impact of Brexit

On 23 June 2016, the British public took to their voting stations to decide on the UK's membership of the European Union. They voted to leave. At time of writing, the implications of this decision are still being processed. The pound has tumbled against both the euro and the dollar, and billions were initially wiped off the stock market. It is believed that the volatility will last for some time, but that some semblance of normality will eventually return to the markets – we just don't know when.

This is an exceptional set of circumstances: not only does the UK want to leave the EU, but David Cameron, prime minister at the time, stepped down, and has been succeeded by Theresa May, formerly the home secretary. She has stated that her government will carry out the public's instruction to leave the EU. At time of writing, the Conservative Party has yet to invoke Article 50 of the Lisbon Treaty, the untested procedure governing how a member state leaves the EU; nor has it indicated how the UK will separate from its friends on the Continent.

It is important to mention Brexit because it has far-reaching implications for the performance of stocks and bonds, for the value of property bought in the UK, and on the UK's standing as a leading economy. It will take months, maybe years, to understand exactly what those implications are. Insiders tell me that while sophisticated traders may attempt to derive short-term gains from the volatility, retail investors are far better off doing nothing and waiting for the markets to stabilize. Sometimes the best advice is an old cliché, and in this case it's: 'Don't just do something, sit there.'

Conclusion

Safety is a relative term. One person's safe haven might be another person's worst nightmare. The best thing an investor can do is to wander along the risk spectrum, stopping where he or she feels comfortable. You'll feel more comfortable if you know your portfolio is diverse, more comfortable yet if your physical investments aren't likely to tank in value because their worth is dependent on pure nostalgia.

Sometimes situations arise that make all investors uncomfortable – in the main, political strife and economic misery. In the months following the referendum, Britain experienced a whole lot of both, and it is not yet clear when the nation will regain its equilibrium. But it won't last forever. Don't make investment decisions out of fear, because you may come to regret them.

Conclusion

Starting safe 02

Safe havens are the places you can park your money with minimum aggravation and be almost guaranteed slow and steady income from that investment. The one thing that makes safe havens stand out from risky ones is this: they are usually not terribly exciting. Weighing up different savings products and tax-free wrappers makes most people want to gouge their eyes out. This is why ordinary people are often put off, but bear with it. Some of the dullest-sounding options are the safest, providing the most reliable rates of return. As George Soros, one of the top 30 richest people in the world, once said: 'If investing is entertaining, if you're having fun, you're probably not making any money. Good investing is boring.'

The thing about safe havens is that they won't make you huge piles of cash. Only big risks can generate big potential returns, but the following strategies can make you more money than if you left £50 notes stuffed in your mattress. It's worth familiarizing yourself with these basics, even if you never progress to the end of the book, where all the bells and whistles are to be found.

Cash: savings products

When it comes to safe havens, straightforward savings accounts are the safest of the safe. Although we are currently in a low-interest-rate environment, there are still gains to be made through these financial products. The government has encouraged us all to save by changing tax rules on the interest we earn on our nest eggs. Did you know that experts recommend that we save 10% of our salary in our twenties, 15% in our thirties, 22% in our forties and 30% in our fifties?

Before April 2016, savers were paying £20 in tax for every £100 of interest they earned, with higher-rate taxpayers losing £40 to the taxman. But now, under the new Personal Savings Allowance (PSA), there is no tax to be paid up to £1,000 a year for basic-rate taxpayers and half that for higher-rate payers. Those paying 45% tax aren't included in the allowance, so their interest is still taxable.

Which savings products does this to apply to? Most of them, excluding share dividends. Cash Isas, which are tax-free, don't count towards the PSA, meaning that you can have both simultaneously earning you interest. Once you cross that £500 or £1,000 PSA limit, however, your usual tax rate kicks in, so it's important to keep an eye on how much you're saving. But it is estimated that 95% of savers in the UK will now have no tax to pay on the interest they make from their savings.

When weighing up the available savings products, it's worth comparing the rate of interest to the interest that you're paying on any loans or overdrafts. It is usually cheaper to pay down debt in the long run than to put your money into a savings product and keep paying that mortgage or longstanding credit card bill. Keep an eye on inflation, too. If the cost of the things you are buying is rising steeply, that also means that the amount you're earning in interest is worth less.

It's much easier to access a decent savings rate than you would think. In fact, some bank current accounts have been known to give a better rate than their dedicated savings accounts. They do this to lure you into becoming a current account holder with them, which means the chance of you taking out a loan or mortgage down the line is much higher. This is why so many high street banks have opted to use this product as a loss leader.

The savings deals on the table

At the moment, the best deals on the market are being offered by Nationwide and TBS, which both offer 5% interest on smaller cash piles (under £2,500 and £2,000 respectively), but these deals are constantly being phased in and out, so use a comparison site such as

MoneySupermarket.com or MoneySavingExpert.com to see the current options.

Many banks offer short-term deals, such as high interest pay-outs for the first six months, on their current accounts. Ideally, you want to stay on top of these deals and move your current account each time the top rate expires. This can be a headache. By being organized and making a list of all regular payments in and out of your current account, you can switch banks every time you're free to access a better deal, and simply check your list for the records that need to be updated. This may require an hour on the phone, but it's an hour that you'll be paid for handsomely down the line. The switching process was made much easier in 2013, when the Current Account Switch Service (CASS) was launched, meaning that it should now take no longer than seven working days to get your new bank account. Other options for the keen saver include: fixed-rate savings; regular savers; and easy-access savings. The interest payable on the latter is usually the lowest, because you can take your money out any time. Regular savers do what they say on the tin: these products pay a decent rate of interest – up to 6% at present – but require the customer to make monthly deposits and may limit the amount you can withdraw from that account. You may need to have a current account with the bank offering the regular saver in order to get access to the deal. Some of the smaller building societies will offer savings products that are open to non-customers, however.

Fixed-rate savings – again, the name says it all. You lock your cash away for a fixed term – up to five years – and you will be paid a fixed rate of interest on that money for the duration. Fixed-rate savings products are probably as risky as they have ever been, due to the fact that interest rates have been so low for so long that there's a higher probability of them rising in the near future. If you're locked into a fixed-rate saver, and the interest rates go sky high, you may only be paid the interest you were promised when you signed up.

Other phrases that are bandied about in the savings world include 'notice savings', which means you have to give notice before accessing your money – around 120 days is standard. Ethical savings, which means the bank or building society promises not to use your money 'for evil', have also soared in popularity. It's an uncomfortable truth that to generate a return high enough to pay a little extra to you and a little bit more back to the bank, some of the investments made by these financial institutions could be on the shadier side.

One thing to be mindful of is that your savings are only covered up to £75,000 by the Financial Services Compensation Scheme (FSCS). This means that if a bank or building society goes bust, that's the maximum that the government will return of your overall savings pot with that institution. This has prompted some savers to split their assets between a number of financial players to minimize the risk. It's worth considering in the wake of some high-profile implosions in the banking sector. Remember Northern Rock, anyone?

Savings hacks

You don't have to open your savings account with a bank that is covered by the FSCS scheme. Indeed, some foreign banks are offering lucrative savings deals, but remember that you opt for one of those at your own risk.

Another question to ask is whether you are the best person in your family to have the savings account. If you are a top-rate taxpayer, and your other half isn't, they could be generating a lot more cash if the account were in their name. This applies only to spouses and should only be considered when there is absolute trust between the two partners, in order to avoid any nastiness down the line.

There is also the option of creating a savings account for your children. A minor can have enough money placed into a savings account in their name to generate £100 in interest each year – and that's per parent. If the money is going into a Junior Isa, you can save up to the current annual Isa limit, which stood at £4,080 in 2016. This is also a great way to get kids interested in saving from a young age, and hopefully encourage them to keep topping up their cash pile when they start making their own money.

Bonds

Bonds are essentially an IOU from a company or a government. Investors lend them money in exchange for a return.

Corporate bonds are loans to big companies that result in annual 'coupons', a fancy word for regular payments at a fixed rate of interest, culminating in a final pay-out of your original investment at the end of the term at some point in the future. These have historically been seen as a safe bet: the only reason they stop paying is if the company goes bust.

Unlike equities, which deliver an average of 5% returns each year – although this can be much higher, bonds are less lucrative.

Nevertheless, for the sake of easy maths, imagine you buy £10,000-worth of 10-year bonds with a 5% return. You will receive £500 each year in interest, and after 10 years you will get your full £10,000 back.

The return from bonds has previously been as high as 3–4% each year over the typical 10-year period, but in the current interest rate environment, with demand for bonds at an all-time high, yields are dropping fast.

Government bonds, or gilts, if they are issued by the UK government, are safer than corporate bonds because it's extremely unlikely that our government will default on its debt. Gilts come in a few shapes and sizes. Dated gilts have a fixed date when they can be cashed in, or 'redeemed', to use industry parlance. Undated gilts or 'perpetuals' are only redeemed on the whim of the government; it can choose to keep paying interest alone forever. One of these perpetual bonds – a war bond – was paying out 8% a year until the government twigged that it was the most lucrative bond on the market and paid it off a few years ago. Conversion gilts are another option, and just mean that one type of gilt can be turned into a different kind of gilt to create market liquidity. At the moment, there's no stamp duty to pay on gilts, and they can be bought and sold through umpteen investment platforms and brokers.

When buying bonds from a broker, it is still preferable to do it over the phone rather than online, as there may be a time lag on the website. Don't be afraid to haggle, because a percentage of a penny difference can have a big impact on your return.

A world of bonds to choose from

You don't have to buy just UK government bonds; there are all sorts out there. For example, you can look at US Treasury bills – or T-bills, municipal bonds – those typically issued by local governments in the United States to fund infrastructure projects. There are also the bonds issued by emerging markets, such as Brazil, South Africa, or the Philippines. Emerging market bonds are riskier than UK government bonds, but you can get better returns. You can also now buy these kinds of bonds in emerging market bundles.

Corporate bonds tend to do badly during recession, while government bonds do well in times of economic strife. When the economy is recovering, corporate bonds do better. Treasury Inflation-Protected Securities (TIPS) are seen as some of the safest bonds you can buy. Invented in 1997, they are made up of US government debt and are protected against inflation, which means that the coupons paid out and the final sum when the bond matures are all adjusted to make sure you don't lose money in a high-inflation environment. These securities pay out twice a year, and can be bought with a minimum investment of $100 over a 5-, 10- or 30-year term. Investors can either buy individual TIPS issued directly or own the securities through a mutual fund. But – another but – a major caveat is that a couple of years ago, there was a sudden and unexpectedly significant decline in the price of TIPS, even though there was no change in the rate of inflation. This was because of 'market technicalities', but the cause is less important than the consequence – a lot of investors were unpleasantly surprised, losing money on their TIPS instead of making it. The lesson: nothing is a sure thing.

Getting into bonds

It is tricky for 'retail investors' – the term used to describe people like you and me – to access a single bond, so most will buy a fund instead, accessing a number of bonds at once. Funds can be a mixture of 200 to 300 different bonds, which is a level of diversification that would be pretty expensive, not to mention difficult, to manage on your own, buying single bonds, one at a time. The chance of default – companies or governments going pop – is also greatly reduced by buying a fund. According to digital wealth manager Nutmeg, the chance of default within a fund stands at around 2%.

Credit ratings agencies, such as Moody's or Standard & Poor's, will give each bond a rating, which ranges from AAA for the most reliable bonds through to BB and even down to C, which means they are highly risky and liable to default. Anything rated BB or below is known as a junk bond. D means the company is already in default. Ratings firms are not infallible, however. A multitude of worthless bonds were rated AAA leading up to the last credit crunch.

Retail bonds are a particular flavour of corporate bond, and have a lower minimum investment than traditional bonds, opening them up to retail investors. While corporate bonds may require a minimum of £100,000, retail bonds can set the bar as low as £1,000. They also tend to pay a higher rate of interest – up to 7%. Retail bonds were launched in 2010 to allow household names to raise money from their customers and fans. Tesco Bank, National Grid and Severn Trent Water have all issued retail bonds.

The London Stock Exchange's retail bond market is called the Order Book for Retail Bonds, so you may see the acronym ORB bandied about. This market means that you don't have to wait for your bond to mature to get your money back: you can trade them to another investor instead. The value of traded bonds may vary. Look out for the terms 'below par' and 'above par' – par just means face value, so above par means they are trading for more than they were originally worth because of investor appetite.

Do your homework

When weighing up bond deals – or even equity deals – you don't have to rely solely on third-party advice: do some digging yourself. Companies that are listed on the stock market have to publish their financial results, and buried in these documents is information about revenue, profits, assets and liabilities. One tip is to take a look at a company's cash flow – the more cash it has to hand, the more likely it is to stay trading – and its interest cover, which refers to the company's ability to meet interest repayments on its debt. The interest cover ratio is calculated by dividing the EBIT – earnings (profits) before interest and taxes – by what the organization spends on interest payments.

Generally, an interest coverage ratio of at least 2 is considered acceptable for a company with a solid, sustainable business, although analysts prefer 3 or more. Don't be afraid to ask the question: 'Hello, I like the look of this bond. What's the company's interest cover ratio?'

The message from investment experts is this: everyone should have some kind of bond in their portfolio. They aren't sexy but they're useful, as a way to maintain a steady income. Equities and bonds are like whisky and water – too much whisky can be risky, so add a little water to help you go the distance.

But are bonds really a safe haven?

Unfortunately, the bond markets are currently in a state of flux, and it is estimated that 17% of all European corporate bonds now trade with a negative yield. Why would you choose to lose money? Well, in the case of some buyers – such as the European Central Bank and the Bank of England – they have no choice. They have to buy bonds for balance sheet and security reasons. But when bonds are in high demand and the market is flooded with buyers, the yields fall.

At the time of writing, bonds issued by 30 governments around the world are trading at a negative yield. Demand for investment-grade bonds is also driving down the yields on retail bonds, leaving investors high and dry. In the short term, this is pushing investors away from mainstream bonds.

How do you know if you're getting a good deal on a bond? Andy Sweeney, who was a bond trader for 15 years, cuts to the chase: 'If I was a private investor calling up a stock broker and asking for a particular bond, the only thing I would want to know is the "yield to maturity"', he says. 'There are loads of other terms out there. Ignore them all.' The 'yield to maturity' is the overall return over the lifetime of the bond. You may see all kinds of other yields quoted – nominal yields, for example – and the coupon may look attractive, but don't be distracted by empty numbers: keep your eye on the prize. Other investment experts agree with this statement. However, according to the CFA Institute, a global association of investment professionals, the gross redemption yield is less useful when applied to funds as opposed to individual bonds:

Higher yields do not necessarily translate into higher realized returns. Yield is not the same thing as total return, and as a matter of fact, higher yields are usually associated with a higher probability of default. The yield-to-maturity calculation that managers use to describe their fund is just that – a description. It's one characteristic of the overall portfolio and is not necessarily a representation of what that fund will earn. The calculation does not assume any change in principal, whether due to defaults or selling prior to maturity, both of which will affect performance.

The only real enemy of bonds is inflation. The rate of interest paid out by bonds stays the same even if inflation soars, eating into your real earnings.

Picking the right bond deal

So what's a decent return? This can be worked out by checking what kind of interest rates are currently being offered for bank accounts, the safest kind of saving method out there. If you can see current accounts advertising 3% returns, it would be foolish to settle for less than 3% on your bond.

'Never look at a bond in isolation', Sweeney says. 'If a bond has been rated AA by Standard & Poor's then look at other bonds rated AA by that agency and see what their returns are. Always check the interest on current accounts and comparatives.'

Compare the costs of investing in different bonds and bond funds through different providers. These will include commission costs, which are fees that are paid to the broker who arranged the deal. Some newly issued bonds may be commission free, because the issuer has absorbed the cost to make them more attractive to investors. There may be an additional fee charged by the brokerage for holding the bonds in your account, which is sometimes called a custody fee. Read the small print to find the hidden costs, too: could you be charged for leaving your account inactive, for example?

Don't be fooled by a bond that is not a bond; mini-bonds, for example, are not safe bets. They are high risk, and they aren't traded, which means you're stuck with them. The point is that the word 'bond' has been synonymous with the word 'safe' since time immemorial; it makes investors all warm and fluffy. Beware pseudo-bonds – did you know that US life insurance policies can be traded, and are known as 'death bonds'? These are not real bonds!

Equities

Nobody can see into the future when it comes to investing in the stock market. Anyone who tells you otherwise is fooling themselves or fooling you.

At its most basic, you are an equity investor if you go to a stock broker and buy a single share in a company. You then either profit from its success or share in its downfall, as the value of your stake fluctuates with the market's reaction to that company's performance. If the company does especially well, it may also issue a dividend, a kind of monetary 'thank you' to investors for holding stock. These are announced – typically with some fanfare – as a pay-out of a certain number of pennies per share.

Betting on the performance of a single company is risky, no matter how robust you believe that business to be. Say you bought a share in Apple. Its products are beloved across the globe – is this a sure bet? What if there were a major fault in one of its gadgets, or its workforce went on strike, shutting down its supply chain? Or what if a rival brought out technology that completely superseded Apple's? Are you still so sure you want to bet on that share? Warren Buffet, arguably the world's most famous investor, famously said: 'The key to investing is found in this rule: buy a share as though you were buying the whole company.' Good companies aren't always good investments. They were good investments in the past, but could well underperform in future. And a good company name doesn't automatically mean a good return.

This is why any equities expert worth his or her salt will tell you never to rely on a single share but to spread your bets across a diversified portfolio of different stocks. A collection of shares, bundled into a single product, is known as a fund. The reason why funds are seen as better than buying shares from a range of companies separately is because you incur much higher fees when you buy them one by one. If you want to buy shares in a foreign company, there may also be foreign exchange costs.

How risky is investing in equities?

We can't see the future but we can look at historic data to see how equities have behaved in the past. According to a recent study by high street bank Barclays, which analysed market data from 1899 to 2013, once the annual return from shares was adjusted for inflation, it stood at a reasonable 5.1% per year for the entire 114-year period.

These results were based on reinvesting everything you made back into the market. If you didn't reinvest the proceeds, your earnings would be substantially lower, just about tracking inflation over time.

Clearly, this means you have to rely on the compounding effect of interest to help boost your overall pot. Barclays' data show that if you had invested £100 in shares in 1899, this would have been worth only £191 by 2013 – this is in real terms, adjusted for inflation, which is the amount that retail prices rose over that time. If, however, all the dividends arising from that initial investment had been reinvested, you would be sitting on a tidy £28,386 over the same period.

Stocks are not a safe haven, as they are at the mercy of the performance of the global economy. Following the referendum, when Britain voted to leave the European Union, investors fled equities in droves. They dragged £3.5 billion out of UK investment funds in June alone, following the vote, according to Hargreaves Lansdown. Industry insiders claim this is substantially more than was pulled out of funds during the last recession. The money slowly trickled back in, but analysts called the financial exodus 'unprecedented'. The money withdrawn from investment funds was funnelled into investments viewed as better able to weather the economic storm – gold funds, dollar funds and utilities were among the principal benefactors. During turbulent times, businesses that depend on discretionary consumer spending – such as fashion retailers and holiday companies – tend to struggle, while those making essentials tend to do better. Tobacco companies have often performed well during times of trouble – perhaps the world smokes more when it's stressed!

How to invest in equities

Getting into the equities market has never been more straightforward, in some ways. There are now thousands of asset managers vying for your business, ranging from traditional financial advisers to online funds and low-cost wealth managers. But this can also be confusing: whom do you trust with your money?

I spoke to experts at the more accessible wealth managers, such as Nutmeg, an online service that lets you start investing with as little as £500, and Vanguard, which has some of the lowest fees in the industry. If you're a beginner with just a few thousand pounds of savings to invest, companies like these make it easy and cheap to get started.

The first step is to save as much as you can, according to Nick Blake, a director at Vanguard. 'It sounds blindingly obvious', he tells me. 'But one of the problems we have in this industry is that of delayed gratification. It's hard to make people save for retirement when you're having fun today.'

He also recommends that anyone investing in equities add some bonds into the mix. Lastly – and of course a low-cost fund manager would say this – keep an eye on the fees that you are paying. The magic of compounding not only helps your pot to grow, it also pumps up the costs of investing. If you are going to invest for 25 years and you are in a fund that costs 2% a year, then, after 25 years, the fund manager will have taken 35% of your money, regardless of how he or she has performed. You have taken all the risk in this scenario, but still end up with only 65% of the proceeds. If you pay 0.2% in costs, you still have 95% of your return after 25 years. A general rule is to be wary of accepting fees of more than 0.9% – the average is around 0.75%.

Don't try to beat the market

Nutmeg's chief investment officer Shaun Port claims that the bigger the range of companies in a particular fund, the better the investment. In layman's terms, if you can't find the needle in the haystack, buy the haystack. He recommends investing in a tracker that is pegged to the performance of an individual market, such as the FTSE – the

UK companies index. These tracker funds have been around since 1975, and remain a popular choice with retail investors. Nutmeg claims that over the long term, trackers always beat individual fund managers.

They are also cheaper. Your typical active fund manager will take a 0.7–1% fee, while a tracker can be as low as 0.1% per year. You pay fees whether the value of your investment rises or falls. Everyone involved in your investment, from the fund platform to the fund manager, will put a hand in your pocket, so always double check exactly what you'll be paying. Everyone knows someone who claims to know an insanely talented fund manager, who always picks the right stocks, but the reality is that this is very rarely the case, and such individuals are almost never consistently right.

When it comes to choosing an index tracker, either you can go for something British, such as a FTSE 100 tracker, or you can look at international options, such as US only, or Chinese. Or you can opt for a global tracker. These are all priced up daily and can be bought direct from a fund manager, or via a discount broker or financial adviser. The risk and reward rules kick in with these trackers. If you choose a tracker that looks at the AIM market, for example, you're looking at much more risk, but the returns are potentially higher, if you're lucky enough to pick the right stocks. Think of AIM as the London Stock Exchange's little brother. He's got lots of potential but is also more liable to fall and scrape his knee.

Avoid being taken in by sensationalist headlines when it comes to buying equities. At the moment, for example, there's a big emphasis on biotech, and investors are piling in en masse. Biotech may indeed be a fast-growing niche, but nothing is certain and an investment into biotech should be balanced out with many other investments. Get the balanced portfolio sorted first, then you can always tilt towards trends from a more solid footing.

Another way to get into equities is through a stocks and shares Isa, which means that you have £15,240 – at the moment – per year to play with tax-free. The best deals on these Isas vary, but online finance supermarkets are pretty good at comparing them side by side. MoneySavingExpert, one of the biggest consumer finance websites, usually has up-to-date information about the options out there.

Equities hacks

Remember that when you own shares in a company, that makes you a shareholder, bringing all kinds of rights. You will have access to financial updates, so you can check on company performance. It's worth familiarizing yourself with the basics of reading a balance sheet. That's a whole book in itself, but there are two overarching rules to bear in mind: if the liabilities – or the debts – are greater than the assets, a company is insolvent, which is bad. And turnover is vanity while profit is sanity. If a company is generating huge sales, that's nice, but for investors to make money they need to make profit. Before any pedants out there point out that that's not always true because loss-making technology companies have also proved very valuable in recent years, that's true. But in most cases, profit really is sanity. As a shareholder, you can attend a company's annual general meeting (AGM) and hear plans for the future, ask questions, and usually have some free tea and biscuits. Your vote, however, is weighted on the amount of the company that you own, so don't expect 0.000001% to go all that far.

Are you an aggressive or a defensive investor?

It's funny how so many of the terms used to describe moving money around would be equally at home on the battlefield. Seventy years ago, Benjamin Graham, one of the 'fathers of value investing' and the man that billionaire Warren Buffet credits for teaching him to become a superstar trader, came up with the definitions for aggressive and defensive investors. He said those who analyse companies and markets in order to buy shares in those with the highest growth potential were aggressive, whereas defensive investors invest less time into stock-picking, instead buying shares from household names that have demonstrated consistently strong financial performance. This was less about appetite for risk, but about experience and the amount of time spent on the process of picking winners.

DIY investing apps

The technology boom of recent years has shaken up every area of our financial lives. We've seen the birth of mobile-only banks, hi-tech services that let you send money between countries without the fat fees of yesteryear, and now personal finance is being targeted by the fintech pioneers.

There are some new investment apps out there that don't just let you play the stock market – crucially, they let you copy the investment strategies of the professionals. Companies such as MeetInvest and GetStocks are out to disrupt the existing investment world and democratize the practice of buying and selling equities.

MeetInvest, which was launched by Swiss entrepreneurs Maria and Michel Jacquemai in 2014, has built algorithms that let you copy the investment strategies of Warren Buffett, James Slater or Sir John Templeton – some of the world's most lauded investment experts.

Registered users choose from a list of gurus on the site, ranging from the big names such as that 'father of value investment' we met earlier, Benjamin Graham, to German former investment fund manager Susan Levermann. Users then choose from 20 strategies, focusing on areas such as spin-off companies, for example – companies born out of universities or big corporations. New gurus and strategies are added regularly, and their strategies are put together using data that are in the public domain. Even if you don't want to invest any money yet, it's a good tool to play with. It's free, after all.

Most of us can't afford a subscription to a Bloomberg terminal ($24,000 a year, if you were wondering). But MeetInvest gathers real-time financial market data on 68,000 stocks worldwide each day, so you can use this library of information to see how your guru's algorithms would perform. The data reach as far back as January 2000. You can reverse formulas to see what would happen if you took the opposite tack. MeetInvest is also a social network, so you can chat to fellow users about their investments, and ask advice on taking the plunge.

Other investment apps creating a buzz include: Robinhood; SigFig; OpenFolio; WealthFront; Finnmason; Kapitall; and Betterment. Some are free, while others claim to offer fee structures that are far lower than traditional brokers.

Or, before you bet cold, hard cash on the market, try it with virtual money instead. Stock Market Simulator is a virtual version of the US stock market, and users can invest imaginary funds to see how they'll fare. Sign up and start with 10,000 virtual bucks – there is a 10–15-minute lag on the real market, which is pretty close to real-time investing. Read up on all these options when you can – it truly is a brave new world out there for the smartphone-savvy investor.

Investing apps for Millennials

GetStocks, which was one of the fastest-growing investment apps in the UK in 2016, has been designed for under-35s who want to make investments in a few swipes. It's one of many investment apps out there, but what makes this version stand out is the ability to subscribe to and follow other investors on the platform, allowing you to see how they have invested their money and to copy those trades.

This is not free. Professional traders charge subscription fees for being able to see which equities they are buying and selling. The average cost to access a portfolio is £10 a month, and you can pay GetStocks to actively mimic all the trades made by your favourite users, specifying your budget. GetStocks makes money on each transaction – typically around £8 a pop.

Like MeetInvest, GetStocks has been designed with some social functionality. Users can see other people's latest tweets and view performance graphs. User data are collated by the app so that when you look at individual stocks, Tesla for example, you can see how many of those holding the electric carmaker's shares also hold Apple stock. This can give an idea of how other investors are behaving.

Another rival to MeetInvest and GetStocks is eToro, which has developed its CopyTrader offering to let users mimic the trades of its top investors. The app allows users to choose from traders who are either trending now, have consistently taken the fewest risks, or are most copied by other investors. eToro relies on the old adage about the wisdom of crowds, and has an estimated 4.5 million traders to choose from.

There are many apps out there aiming to help ordinary people access the stock market for the first time. Acorns is one of the more innovative ideas. It plugs in to your credit or debit card and rounds up each purchase to the nearest dollar, investing the change into one of five diversified investment portfolios. If you buy a coffee for £2.99, that penny (adjusted for currency rate) will be invested into a port-folio, ranging from conservative (low risk, low reward) to aggressive (high risk, high reward).

These portfolios have been assembled with guidance from Nobel Prize-winning economist and 'father of modern portfolio theory', Dr Harry Markowitz. Students can invest for free, which helps explain why three-quarters of users are between 18 and 34. Non-students pay $1 per month or 0.25% per year, depending on the size of the investment budget.

At the time of writing, Acorns has 850,000 active accounts and has raised around $62 million in funding from the likes of PayPal. Co-founder Jeff Cruttenden told TechCrunch that 'all our portfolios have outperformed the S&P on a risk-adjusted return basis', but it's still early days for the app.

There is a reason why these apps are becoming so popular: talking to a financial adviser can be frightening. If you haven't grown up talking about stocks and shares, there's a presumption that you'll be made to feel stupid. Apps put you in control, and no one ever worries that an app will judge their decision. That said, some human beings learn best from other human beings. Don't be frightened of speaking to investment experts. Most will be happy to help and are the first to admit that this stuff is complicated.

Exchange-traded funds

Don't be put off by the dull-sounding name. Exchange-traded funds (ETFs) are being hailed as the future of the investment industry by some insiders, because they are one of the cheapest and easiest ways to get a completely diversified portfolio. They are a member of the exchange-traded product (ETP) family, which all basically aim to replicate the performance of a market.

An ETF is a fund that tracks the performance of an index, just like a FTSE 100 or S&P 500 tracker, only it too can be bought and sold, like a share in a company. If you buy a FTSE 100 ETF, you are effect-ively hedging your bets and buying a tiny piece of all 100 companies. There are also ETFs for corporate bonds, which typically contain more than 200 individual bonds, reducing the risk of default.

Imagine that you want to make a particular meal. You can go out and buy all the ingredients individually, or you can buy a recipe box, with everything you need to make the meal, in the amounts required. The recipe box is a bit like the ETF.

ETFs have all the best bits of a fund, combining a wide variety of companies or markets, which can be hard to access one by one, and the best bits of a share, too. They are available to buy at any time during the day, unlike index funds, which have a delay before you can trade.

The cost of an ETF that tracks a developed equity market, such as the FTSE 100, will be pretty low – around 0.1% from some wealth managers. Once all the costs are accounted for, you're usually looking at paying out around 0.5%. This compares favourably to an actively managed fund, which can cost up to 2%.

Source, one of the largest providers of ETFs in Europe, recently polled 55 of its biggest investors to find out their appetite for these funds. The institutional investors said that they expected the ETF market to double in size over the next five years, and eventually to account for 6% of global investment fund assets under management. That's a pretty meaty chunk of the market. As for how much of your wealth you should hold in ETFs or other passive/index-linked funds, these guys opt for around 8% of the total investable pot.

How to invest in ETFs

When looking to invest in an ETF, you should check out its Total Expense Ratio (TER). This shows the total cost to the investor, taking into account all the fees charged. This is shown as a percentage, and you want that percentage to be as low as possible. Many ETFs should pay you a generous income, more than 5% in some cases.

There is also no stamp duty to pay when you invest in ETFs, al-though rules may change in the future. Some wealth managers charge trading fees, while some of the newer, online players, such as Nutmeg, have stripped out these costs to allow people to invest smaller sums of money – as little as £500.

Another interesting point about ETFs is that they can be incorporated into your Self-Invested Personal Pension (Sipp). This is a DIY pension that you manage yourself. ETFs are not new – they've been around since 1993 – so they are a tried and tested way of investing, and there are now more than 2,000 ETFs listed on the London Stock Exchange.

ETFs are also passive investments, meaning that you don't have to pay a fund manager to pull levers in order to make money. They just do their thing. Of course, ETF returns are limited by their very nature: it's difficult to outperform a market when you were created to track it.

Not all ETFs are created equal, however. The most common type actually buys a tiny chunk of the companies or bonds found in the index that it's tracking. This is known as 'physically replicating', and this type is generally seen as a safer breed of ETF, especially when tracking the major indices. But there is another kind. These ETFs use 'derivatives', complex financial instruments, to mimic the performance of the index. They have their own weird rules, known as a 'synthetic investment strategy'. This can be as dodgy as it sounds, and can carry high risks because these ETFs may not perform the way you expect. Be careful, too, of those that focus on strange assets that investors may struggle to find data about. These could be more unpredictable in the event of a financial crisis.

Mutual funds

Mutual funds, like ETFs, are also open-ended investments, meaning that you can get your money out at any time. The 'mutual' just means there are many investors, and their combined cash will be used to buy securities, such as equities or bonds or other market instruments. Mutual funds are run by a professional manager, and – like ETFs – give small investors access to diversified portfolios.

There are around 8,000 mutual funds out there at the time of writing, all specializing in different things (large-caps, small-caps, municipal bonds, distressed assets – you name it), involving different fees and costs. A good rule of thumb is to look for a low TER, which means a higher chance of beating the market. Also, watch out for high turnover ratios – these can be bad news. A 100% turnover ratio means that positions are held for an average of one year on average; 200% means six months, and so on. The higher the turnover ratio, the higher the trading costs – although it's worth reading the small print to make sure. As with any product of this nature, beware managers showing off stellar performance statistics. Past performance does not predict future results.

How to pick the right mutual fund

To get an independent take on the mutual funds out there, check out Morningstar or Trustnet. These are free, online data services that independently rank funds. Morningstar lets you compare funds based on what kind of securities they bet on, their returns – even the fund manager's tenure. Check out its FundInvestor 500, which is a ranking of the top 500 mutual funds. In the wake of the Brexit vote, this ranking helped investors to work out the safest havens amid all the market volatility. It was the mutual funds focusing on gold, investment-grade corporate bonds and US municipal bonds that performed best in the aftermath. Another useful resource is the Association of Investment Companies (AIC), which lets you find and compare its 400 global members.

There are three types of mutual fund: unit trusts, open-ended investment companies (OEICs) and closed-ended funds. The phrase 'unit trust' makes it sound highly complicated, but it just means a fund that is filled with bonds or shares by a fund manager and then split into units. This is what you're buying. The fund manager can create new units every time an investor wants to buy into the fund and cancel units for those selling out of the fund. OEICs are practically the same as unit trusts except that they are structured like a company, creating and cancelling shares rather than units when investors buy in or cash out. Closed-ended funds are most commonly known as investment trusts in the UK. More on these in a moment.

The return from an equities fund depends on whether that selection of companies beats the market as a whole. In an absolute return fund, investors are promised good returns no matter what the market conditions. That usually involves making some pretty risky bets, using leverage, shorting stocks and so on. A note about these – no fund can promise you 'absolute returns', not really, and in 2016, six out of the ten worst-performing UK funds were – you guessed it – absolute return funds. Be wary of guarantees in the world of investing: they are rarely what they seem.

Investment trusts

Unlike open-ended funds, ETFs and index trackers, investment trusts are 'closed-ended' – an awkward phrase that just means they hold a fixed amount of money. With mutual funds, in contrast, capital can flow in and out of the pot. When an investment trust is created, it issues a fixed number of shares that are publicly listed, like a company on the London Stock Exchange.

The word 'trust' is actually misleading, and is another example of how the financial system has evolved to confuse and befuddle outsiders. It's not really a trust, which is defined as when one person or party holds an asset on behalf of another person for their benefit. Trust just means 'company' in this case.

In an investment trust, the investors' money is pooled and will then be put into a wide range of stocks and shares. These can be incredibly varied, from African food producers to commercial property. These trusts tend to make longer-term, more esoteric investments, such is the nature of the beast.

But here's where it gets a little more confusing. The assets in the investment trust have a value, which is published every day, and is known as the net asset value. But the share price is traded on an exchange, which means there can be a difference between the actual value of the investment trust and the amount that it is worth to investors trading shares in it.

Imagine that the trust specializes in residential property, and investors are worried that there will be a house price crash. Even though it hasn't happened yet, and may not happen, the shares may start to sell at a discount. The value of the property owned by the trust hasn't fallen at all, but the market sentiment taints the investment anyway.

This is important, because to get out of an investment trust there has to be another buyer, and you're basically held hostage to the price on that day. If there are more sellers than buyers, share prices will fall and fall. On the flipside, shares can also trade at a premium.

Are investment trusts really a safe haven?

Some wealth managers are less fond of investment trusts because of the lack of liquidity in the market; if their customers suddenly want their money back, it can be hard to extract. An investment trust is structured like a company in its own right, so the price of shares depends on the market and will vary with demand. The more popular it is, the higher the price, which means that investors are paying more than the underlying assets are actually worth – and vice versa. But investment trusts are hailed as strong products by other experts because they give the regular Joe access to a range of diverse and varied investments. In an environment where a diverse portfolio is a must, this is seen as a significant benefit.

As for the returns, Morningstar, the online investing portal, publishes a ranking of the top performers. At the time of writing, the top investment trusts are focused either on private equity, emerging markets – Asia Pacific, excluding Japan, and Latin America, mainly – or UK equities and bonds. Investors are paid a dividend, just like those investing directly in a company. The fund manager may take a performance fee, so the better your investment does, the higher their pay-out. Trust managers can stockpile dividend reserves, and spread out dividend payments, to ensure that the money you're paid keeps rising steadily, instead of experiencing peaks and troughs. This means that investors can still make decent money in hard times. According to data seen by the *Daily Telegraph*, during the 2008 financial crisis, when company profits collapsed, 11 out of the 14 top trusts paid a growing dividend throughout the downturn, with two holding the dividend at the same level and one cutting it. Recent data from the AIC have shown that investment trusts outperform funds in 10 out of 15 sectors over multiple time periods, from one to ten years.

A bit of trivia: the first investment trust was invented by the Foreign & Colonial Investment Trust in 1868 'to give the investor of moderate means the same advantages as the large capitalists in diminishing the risk of spreading the investment over a number of stocks'. F&CIT was launched by Philip Rose, the same guy who founded the Royal Brompton Hospital in London's Kensington.

How to choose an investment trust

To work out whether the investment trust you're interested in is in rude health, one tip is to look at the 'dividend cover', which is the amount by which the dividend is exceeded by earnings. If you see a cover of 100%, that means the dividends match earnings precisely. As the percentage falls below 100%, the dividend is becoming increasingly 'uncovered', which means it could prove unsustainable over the long term, and a riskier investment.

The issue with trusts is their level of gearing – the amount of money that the fund manager borrows against the investment trust's assets, because they think they can beat the stock market and want to amplify the gains. If this bet goes bad, the losses are amplified instead.

Fund supermarkets

There are a number of online players that allow investors to mix and match a range of unit trusts, investment trusts, shares, bonds, ETFs, OEICs and more through a single account. These are known as fund supermarkets, or sometimes 'platform', 'fund shop', 'fund broker' or 'investment shop'. Notice how so many terms start to sound the same when speaking the language of money?

These supermarkets have become very popular in recent years because they offer such a wide choice of funds – more than a single provider will have on its books. They are also frequently cheaper – although not always. The explosion of fund supermarkets created a sort of price war with traditional providers, not unlike the price wars between actual high street supermarkets, which has driven down fees in the same way that it has halved the price of milk.

The advantage of choosing a fund supermarket is that you can manage your account online yourself, and log in whenever you want to check the status of your investments. However, heed the warning from the beginning of the book – it's rarely a good idea to spend hours agonizing over small price movements. Come up with a strategy to diversify your portfolio, execute it, then leave it alone.

The other thing that investors like about these platforms is that you can put these investments inside a tax-efficient wrapper, such as a stocks and shares Isa or Sipp. There is no capital gains tax on any investment profits within either Isas or Sipps and no further tax to pay for higher-rate taxpayers at the moment.

Among the popular fund supermarkets are: AJ Bell Youinvest, Bestinvest, Charles Stanley Direct, Fidelity, Hargreaves Lansdown, TD Direct Investing and The Share Centre. These vary from 'no frills' to premium, and will come with very different fees and charges.

How to choose a platform

When you buy a fund direct from a fund provider, you may pay an initial charge of up to 5%. Fund supermarkets often waive this sign-up fee completely. Instead, they make their money through annual fees and dealing fees. The annual fee can be a fixed amount, such as £100 a year, or can be charged as a percentage of the value of all the funds you hold through your accounts, say 0.25%.

Check for a cap on the percentage fees, otherwise you could get stung for serious money as your investments grow. Dealing fees are paid every time you buy or sell a fund, and are usually a flat fee of up to £10. To lure in new customers, fund supermarkets may make a lot of noise about how they let you trade for free – just make sure you're not paying a whopper of an annual charge. The funds themselves may charge their own management fees too; typically 0.75% a year.

Most fund supermarkets will also charge exit fees – see how all these little amounts start to add up? – and these can be as much as £25 for every fund you hold in your portfolio. Check for other hidden fees, such as a charge for certain kinds of product – buying shares often comes with these extra charges, while buying a fund may not.

The charges also vary depending on the size of your investment. If you have a £5,000 pot, it may be a good idea to go with platform X, but that same fund shop could be the worst choice for someone with

£15,000, who'd be much better off with platform Y. The *Daily Telegraph*'s Money section frequently updates a ranking of the top fund supermarkets in the UK, and the costs for investors with as little as £5,000 and as much as £1 million to invest.

Its latest chart showed that AJ Bell Youinvest and Strawberry were the best bets for those on the smallest budgets, Charles Stanley Direct has the most favourable rate for £100,000, and pots of £500,000 were best served by James Hay Modular iPlan.

You'll need to do your homework and compare several different funds before signing up. That's just the beginning. In the trade, the term to describe someone who picks their own stocks and shares in this way is 'execution only' – you'll get no help from the platform, you're on your own. You'll need to wade through more than 1,000 investment options and work out what you actually want to invest in – no one said DIY investing was easy.

Premium Bonds

Premium Bonds are a National Savings & Investments savings product that pays out interest based on the results of a lottery. Draws are held each month, and every bond has an equal chance of winning, so technically the more you have, the greater your chance of landing some cash.

These bonds were first introduced by Harold Macmillan in the 1956 Budget to help control inflation and encourage savings after the Second World War. The very first bond was sold on 1 November 1956. Harold Wilson, who succeeded Macmillan as prime minister, opposed their introduction, calling Premium Bonds a 'squalid raffle'.

Historically, Premium Bonds were an easy place to park your savings, without paying any tax. Unlike other savings products that lock up your money, you can withdraw your cash whenever you want. They appeal to the gambler inside all of us: will I be a winner?

These are still the UK's most popular savings product, even in an environment where many other savings products are tax-free. It is estimated that more than 21 million people are currently holding some £80 billion in bonds.

The maximum you can hold in Premium Bonds is £50,000, and the minimum spend is £100. But should you buy them?

Premium Bonds can make a fun gift for children – although it's worth noting that bondholders must be over 16, so must be put in a parent's name until then. NS&I even has a cutsie name for the machine that selects the winning numbers each month. Your fate will be in the hands of Ernie (Electronic Random Number Indicator Equipment)! But the likelihood of winning is extremely low. According to MoneySavingExpert, the odds of getting even £25 are 1 in 30,000, rising to 1 in 30,249,250,802 for £1 million.

How much can you make from Premium Bonds?

In June 2016, the average pay-out for Premium Bonds dipped from £1.35 for every £100 to £1.25. Compare this to the 1.4% interest you could earn on an easy-access Isa, for example. But even this 'average' is misleading. This suggests that everyone gets £1.25 for every £100 invested, which is impossible as the minimum pay-out is £25. Instead of using the 'mean' average, the truth is closer to the median.

If 1 million people gave you an apple, and at the end of the month you gave a single person all 1 million apples, the mean average pay-out would be one apple – but not everyone got an apple. Using the median method, if all those people lined up and you asked the person halfway down the queue if they'd won, the likelihood is that they hadn't. This makes the median a big fat zero. Heed the cautionary tale of Paddy Dewey, who decided to invest £100 in Premium Bonds in August 1969. Over the following 40 years, she didn't win a single penny. If she had invested it in equities, it would have been worth £843 in real terms.

If you do win, however, the prize is tax-free. Since the launch of the PSA in April 2016, this is less of a lure. The PSA means that all savings interest is now automatically tax-free (excluding those paying top-rate 45% tax who are not included in the allowance), unless you're earning more than £1,000 interest a year (as a basic 20% taxpayer) or more than £500 interest a year (as a higher earner on a 40% or more tax rate). This all but kills the tax advantage – although Premium Bonds don't count towards PSA, so it can be considered an extra allowance.

The enemy of the Premium Bond, however, is inflation. If inflation rises, the value of the money held in bonds stays the same – unless you're winning, which we've established is unlikely. As the value of the pound falls in the real world, your frozen bonds are actually losing money, in real terms.

Premium Bonds do, however, benefit from the magic of compounding – if you do win, and leave your winnings in the account as bonds, your chances of winning again go up.

Another important point: if you die, your Premium Bonds can't be passed on. They will remain active, and eligible to win, for 12 months after the bondholder dies, but you must cash them in during this period. Prizes that were won before the bondholder died can be claimed at any time but may be subject to Inheritance Tax.

NS&I will attempt to contact you if you've won, but bondholders who move house and don't update their records may not get the message, so it's important to log in and check to see if you've won. There is around £50 million in unclaimed prizes sitting in the pot right now, so dust off that old certificate of investment and check.

Residential property

There are ways to invest in residential property without becoming a buy-to-let landlord or living in the house yourself. You can invest in a fund or platform that takes care of the buying, selling, and everything in between.

This means that you don't have to stump up the cash for a whole house; you can just invest a small percentage of the pot, and you don't have to worry about tenants and broken boilers. One example of a company that claims to democratize the world of residential property investment is Property Partner. Founded in 2014 and open for business since 2015, it operates a crowdfunding model, allowing armchair investors to put money into investments they like. These backers then receive shares in that property, like buying stock in a company.

Property Partner buys the property with investors' money alongside debt, and issues a monthly dividend as income, which is generated from the rents paid by the tenants. It takes a management fee for its trouble. After five years, investors get the option to sell, and can receive their whole original stake back – possibly with a significant profit, if the property has increased in value.

The minimum investment is £50, and the company currently has £60 million worth of property on its books, although about half of this is tied up in mortgages, not equity.

Is residential property a safe haven?

Property schemes have previously been frowned upon because they are illiquid. What if there's a property crash? Investors trying to get their money out of commercial property developments in 2008 know only too well the trauma of finding themselves locked into an investment that's losing value by the second. In 2016, £650 million worth of property developments were scrapped after the Brexit vote in London alone, while property funds haemorrhaged £1.4 million in June as investors scrambled to secure their capital, fearing a crash. Property Partner does run a secondary market, which allows its backers to trade shares and should in theory provide more liquidity, although it hasn't been tested by a downturn yet. Investing in residential property should always be a long-term investment. According to Property Partner, five years is the ideal amount of time. If Property Partner are to be believed, since 1973, there has not been a single five-year period when an investment in residential property would have given you a negative return. So the chances of selling at market value in five years and being worse off are fairly unlikely – not impossible but unlikely. Other property crowdfunding platforms are Property Moose, The House Crowd and Property Crowd, which all have a different focus. The reason why this kind of crowdfunding is being treated as less risky than other kinds is that investments are held against a physical asset. Property Partner says its returns stand closer to 10% per year, as a mixture of dividend payments and capital growth.

Other options for investing in residential property

There are couple of other ways of investing in residential property without owning the bricks and mortar yourself. Castle Trust, which matches people seeking a mortgage with investors looking for returns, is another operator in this space. It used to offer a Housa product, which tied returns to the performance of the housing market, but this is not currently available.

Hearthstone UK Residential Property is an example of a specialist tax structure called a Property Authorized Investment Fund (PAIF). Investors can put money into PAIFs through their Isa now, making these investments more tax efficient, especially compared to a unit trust investing in property. Hearthstone claims to have delivered returns of 11% to investors during 2015.

If you're considering putting your money into a company that will invest in residential property, you want to know that it's buying the right kind of homes. Stock should be near transport hubs – particular attention is currently being paid to sites near Crossrail stations, for example. The area needs to be attracting investment from other companies, too, and to have a strong local economy. Avoid towns where the majority of workers are dependent on a single employer, and places that have posted consistently weak growth compared to the national average. The ideal residential property is freehold, and comes in an unbroken block – a whole apartment building, not a few flats in a larger development. This is for two reasons: the first is that you typically get a discount when buying all the flats in one building at once. This is known as 'investment value'. The second point is that the company that owns the whole building controls its destiny – it can choose to split it up and sell off parts, or offer shared ownership. This becomes more complex with multiple stakeholders clamouring for their own way. The property fund that you back should have an experienced management team that knows all of this already, but it's worth asking the right questions to keep them on their toes. London is seen as a riskier place to buy property now, despite the high demand, because growth in rental values has not kept pace with house prices, so you're making a big bet for a small win. Regional property investments tend to generate a higher income return.

The reason why residential property is seen as a solid investment is that everyone needs somewhere to live. Commercial property is much more subject to the vagaries of the economy. After the last financial crisis, commercial property values almost halved but residential fell by a more muted 18%.

Commercial property

Commercial property is another way for investors to diversify their portfolios and reduce risk, because the performance of property prices isn't highly correlated to other asset classes, such as equities. That said, when the 2008 recession hit, schemes to build towering office buildings were abandoned and investors lost a lot of money. Commercial property prices fell 44% almost overnight following the financial crash in the United States.

Commercial property broadly refers to three types of building: shops, offices or industrial property, such as warehouses and factories. Commercial property is sometimes seen as being less risky than residential because the leases are much longer, up to 15 years, and there tends to be less risk of default. But it is harder to get an interest-only mortgage on a commercial property than on a buy-to-let property.

According to data from Legal & General Property (LGP), more than £60 billion was invested into the commercial property markets in 2014, up from £52 billion the previous year. It also found that commercial property prices rose nearly 20% between 2014 and 2015, while rents rose 9% in London over the three years to 2015, and 2% outside the capital. LGP is forecasting growth of 2.8% on average each year from 2016 to 2018.

Is it really a safe haven?

One of the drivers of market growth is the lack of available office space. In 2010, there were empty offices and shops all over the UK. Commercial property availability peaked that year. Since then, the number of vacant offices and shops across the UK has fallen by 28% as businesses expanded again. There is also a shortage of space because so much commercial property has been turned into homes; it is estimated that in 2014 alone, around 6 million square feet of office space in England was converted from office to residential use.

Commercial property produces two kinds of income – the monthly rental income from occupying businesses, and capital growth as the value of the property rises.

There are three ways to invest in commercial property. You can do it directly, buying an office building, for example, but this may cost many tens of millions. Smaller investors on limited budgets usually invest in direct commercial property funds to access the market. These are structured like unit trusts, OEICs or investment trusts, and will buy properties on behalf of multiple investors. Real Estate Investment Trusts (REITs) boast tax benefits over other property funds because REITs don't pay Corporation Tax as long as 90% of profits are paid out as dividends to investors. The other way to profit from the performance of commercial property without physically owning bricks and mortar is to buy into an indirect fund, packed with property companies. This tends to be more risky and doesn't help to diversify risk in the portfolio as well as the old-fashioned purchase of property, because you're essentially just buying shares.

Commercial property vs buy-to-let

Commercial property is less hands-on than buy-to-let because the business that occupies the building is in charge of refurbishing and maintaining it. With residential property, the landlord has to be hands-on, fixing any issues that arise and keeping on top of wear and tear. Tenancies in the residential world can change every six months, which means a lot of paperwork. Another reason that commercial property may trump residential buy-to-let is that reforms to the stamp duty regime mean that 90% of commercial property owners are forecast to pay less tax. The previous Chancellor of the Exchequer, George Osborne, brought in new rules to charge a different rate for each band of the property's value instead of a standard flat rate, which the Treasury claimed would leave the majority of commercial property owners better off.

You don't have to focus on UK commercial property; there are opportunities to buy sites overseas. BrickVest is one fund that is focused on buying shops on secondary high streets in France, Germany and Scandinavia. Investments start at 1,000 euros.

A note about another kind of commercial property: car park schemes were touted as great investments following the financial crash. It was claimed that investors could purchase spaces in car park developments, which would later be sold for a decent return. Park First is one of the more transparent providers out there, and owns off-airport car parks at major UK airports, including London Gatwick. It promises that investors will receive an 8% return in years one and two, rising to a predicted 10% in years three and four, and 12% in years five and six. This sounds like a good deal, but investors should always be wary of 'guaranteed returns' – there are never any guarantees. What if no one wants to buy the car park?

Gold and bullion

Think of gold as 'wealth insurance'. Gold comes into its own when all your other investments start tanking – it's the counterbalance to equities, for example. Gold is also one of the assets of 'last resort', alongside diamonds. If the unthinkable happened, and there was a financial apocalypse, or the banking system failed, or the economy was subject to hyperinflation – wheelbarrows full of cash to buy a single load of bread, that sort of thing – the value of gold would soar.

Gold is a preferable asset of last resort to silver, say, because it is very valuable in small quantities; holding £10,000 in silver would be a very heavy rucksack.

It is advisable to hold no more than 10% of your wealth in gold – recommendations range from 5% to 20%, so this is the happy medium. You mustn't expect a return from it, as you would other investments. By 'wealth insurance', we mean that it will only become valuable at a time when you're haemorrhaging money on your other investments, which you don't want to happen. Most people end up never selling their gold, but pass it on to family, as their insurance policy.

Is gold really a safe haven?

Gold prices have been extremely volatile across the past decade. In 2006 and 2007, canny investors who suspected an imminent financial crash began stockpiling gold, and its price rocketed by a third. In 2008, when the banking crisis was entrenched, gold's value rose a further 25%, and its spot price – the price at which physical gold could be bought – traded above $1,000 an ounce for the first time, hitting an all-time high of $1,030.80 in March 2008.

Gold remained a safe haven all throughout the financial crisis, with its price rising as new economic shocks emerged, hitting $1,282 in September 2010. Its price peaked in late 2011, at $1921.50, when Greece was about to be turfed out of the eurozone, and that's when the precious metal began to lose its lustre.

Gold isn't the only safe haven out there – the lure of the US dollar is also incredibly powerful during a downturn. And with economic growth returning in the United States, the dollar became even more attractive.

Gold has lost more than half its value over the past four years, and some analysts have even revoked its safe haven status, claiming that it is a risky commodity. But gold has only done what it always does in times of plenty – it loses value. Lest we forget, Gordon Brown famously sold off more than half (58% to be precise) of the nation's reserves of gold bullion between 1999 and 2002 for just $200 per ounce, a record low, during a time when the UK's economy was growing steadily. This is why investors need to take a long, long, long-term view on gold.

Should you buy gold now?

Interestingly, in 2015 Rob Halliday Stein, the millionaire founder of BullionByPost, one of the biggest physical gold vendors in the UK, began personally buying gold sovereigns after five years of buying no gold at all. He bought in at £720 an ounce ($1,049), and by January 2016 the price was at £760. Following the referendum vote to leave the European Union, prices rose yet higher, to more than £1,000.

In the wake of the UK's 2016 vote to leave the European Union, the price of gold spiked almost instantly, rising from £838 per ounce on 23 June to £983 literally overnight. The number of online searches for the phrase 'buy gold' surged by 500% as soon as the leave result became likely at around 5 am on 24 June, according to Google.

The gold price peaked at a three-year high of £1,062 in July 2016 before plateauing. But if the uncertainty around Brexit – and other worrying global events, such as the ongoing terrorist attacks – dissipates, the price is likely to fall. This means it's probably not the best time to start buying gold – you'll pay a premium.

Investors looking to hold some of their wealth in gold are faced with several options: gold funds; shares in gold mining companies; bullion; and gold coins. Looking at the historic performance of all of these options, it is bullion and coins that have delivered the most solid performance.

When the value of gold falls, the market capitalization of the companies mining for the stuff tends to fall far lower – bad news for the investor. And while the price of bullion fell 35% between 2011 and 2014, the losses posted by funds focused on gold were far greater: every fund more than halved, with some losing even more.

Even when buying physical gold, the investor has to think carefully. Some gold coins – Britannias and sovereigns – are exempt from Capital Gains Tax (CGT) in the UK. However, this means they are sold at a premium of around 2%. It's probably not worth buying these coins unless you're investing more than £30,000. You can do the maths yourself to work out which deal works better for you, weighing that 2% premium against either the basic CGT rate of 18%, or the higher rate of 28% paid by wealthier taxpayers.

If you're putting £10,000 into gold, you're better off buying gold bars. You can either store your gold in your own safe deposit box, or use a third party. Do your homework if doing the latter – BullionByPost uses Brink's, which has been accredited by the likes of the London Bullion Market Association.

When buying physical gold, you also need to make doubly sure that you're using a reputable vendor. Check out their accounts on Companies House, a free service provided by the UK government, to make sure they are a registered business. Remember the old adage: if a deal looks too good to be true, it probably is. There are unscrupulous companies promising bargain basement prices – if you read a deal that says, 'Buy gold out of the mine today for this low, low price and we will deliver it to you in six months', run for the hills.

Ultimately, gold is a hard asset that is ruled by the laws of supply and demand. It is a metal that is used in the manufacture of electronics and in dentistry, and remains the metal of choice for a large proportion of jewellery. All of these industrial users require the physical product, not a piece of paper, so when demand outpaces supply, the price will rise. This is why some traders believe that small investors are best off owning the metal itself, rather than playing in ones and zeros, such as in futures markets, which are dominated by big institutional traders.

Conclusion

Most investors will limit themselves to the investment options outlined in this chapter. You want to hold as much of your wealth in high-performance savings products as you can, tax-free, and hold a mix of bonds and equities on top.

According to an analysis by JP Morgan, the bank, investors with a basic portfolio made up of half bonds and half equities would never have lost money in any 10-year period since 1950.

Shares should always be viewed as long-term investments, as they are more of a gamble in the near term. Don't forget that investing though a tax wrapper, such as your Isa, is the best way to preserve your return.

There are many ways to invest in these equities, from actively managed mutual funds to passive trackers and ETFs. Work out what kind of equity investing works for you, but remember that a good spread of different investments is more important than each individual one. As Aristotle once said: 'The whole is greater than the sum of its parts.'

To diversify your portfolio further, you could add some property to the mix, and perhaps a little gold, just to be on the safe side.

It can't be stressed enough that diversification is the only route to safety. Buying a single share in a company is phenomenally risky on its own, as is piling all your capital into gold. In many ways, it is disingenuous to talk about safe havens at all – a lot of the safety comes down to timing. If you buy and sell at the right point in the cycle, any investment can appear to be safe.

Getting riskier 03

This is the point when the investment opportunities get a little more edgy. We're leaving behind the safer havens and looking at options where the possibility of losing your money rises slightly. These aren't foolish investments, but you have to be more careful.

This is also the part of the book devoted to more of the physical investments – where you actually buy and hold items in the hope that they will increase in value. This can be appealing – the collector inside all of us longs to own items that appreciate. But they also come with distinct downsides. Most physical investments don't pay an income, unlike traditional financial investments. You have to be very sure you've bought the right things, store them carefully and insure them in case anything goes wrong. Nevertheless, some investors find putting a small proportion of their cash into physical assets very rewarding. For investors looking to dabble in property, there are also a few more options to investigate here.

Student housing

Back in 2012, there was a perfect storm in the student housing market. Universities were allowed to charge tuition fees of up to £9,000. Student visa rules were tightened to prevent abuse of the system, and university grade boundaries were toughened up. It was feared that this triptych of challenges would decimate demand for student accommodation, but while there was a softening in the market, it was a short-lived blip.

According to official data, full-time student numbers in 2014 were almost back at 2010 levels. There may be fewer UK undergraduates these days, but the shortfall has been made up by overseas students, driven by the removal of the cap on the number of people that can come to the UK to study. Not all universities are created equal, and the bottom-tier institutions have struggled. Young people want to know that they are not spending thousands of pounds and taking on serious debt for a second-class degree. They are fussier about courses and tend to care more about things such as graduate employability in that university city. Top universities are faring well in this environment: UK undergraduate numbers at the top 20 institutions edged up by 1.4% on the previous year in 2014, according to the Complete University Guide.

Why student housing?

Student numbers are steady and the student housing market has quietly been morphing into a powerful asset class. This is because getting new developments off the ground is actually pretty tricky, owing to planning constraints, which means that demand usually outstrips supply. When new opportunities come up, they are snapped up by eager investors.

According to property company Savills, 74,500 beds were traded in 2015, generating a value of £5.9 billion. To put this into context, it compares to £2.4 billion a year, on average, between 2012 and 2014. This steep growth curve is a little misleading, because several big developments hit maturity at once, and others were restructured, allowing overseas investors to pile in.

The thing that investors really like about student accommodation is that there's a reliable, recurring revenue stream – rents come in every month – and the value of the property tends to rise over time. It's a win–win. Student accommodation also tends to be counter-cyclical, so it performs well when other investments aren't.

How does the humble private investor get into this market? The truth is that it's very difficult. You can go direct, buy a student house and get your House in Multiple Occupation (HMO) licence – you need one of these if you're renting to five or more people who are living in three storeys or more and sharing some facilities. Or you can invest in student property schemes. Companies such as Select Property, which builds high-end accommodation for wealthy overseas students (as well as some more affordable housing), promise investors returns of up to 7%. This way, you don't have to worry about broken boilers and noise complaints because there is a middleman who actually manages the property, and you can sell your room(s) to another investor if you need to; you're not locked in. There are also Real Estate Investment Trusts (REITs), which are modelled on mutual funds and allow investors to make a regular income while holding a diversified portfolio of student digs. An exchange-traded fund (ETF) focused on this market is another option. Alternatively, you could buy shares in the bigger student housing developers, such as Unite, but remember that putting all your eggs into one basket always carries much more risk.

Where are the student housing hotspots?

Insiders advise looking at student towns and cities where the student accommodation offering is still undeveloped. Take Bath. The amount of purpose-built student housing has risen in recent years, but the demand-to-supply ratio still stands at 2.5, which means that around 60% of the 19,600 full-time students who attend the city's two universities have to find a bed elsewhere. Conversely, Liverpool, which has quite a significant amount of purpose-built student accommodation, with over 20,000 beds available in university and private schemes, still has 2.1 students for every available bed. The key here would be to find a central location, or a development very near the campus, which could give these digs an advantage over other developments.

London is an obvious market but there are some issues here. Student housing developers are vying with residential, commercial and other student property developers over the same sites. It's a dogfight. London currently has around 3.2 full-time students for every bed, with a projected 17,000 beds in development, taking the ratio to 2.6. Central London property is monstrously expensive, but there may be value in buying sites along some of the London Underground and Overground lines. According to Savills, the best places to find rising rents are Brighton, Bournemouth, Cardiff, Southampton and Coventry, but Scottish university towns are a riskier investment, as they tend to have a stronger domestic market, and local students have less of a need for purpose-built student accommodation. For the gutsy investor, there are also more and more deals being done in Europe, where the market is much less developed. Sector specialists The Student Housing Company, Victoria Hall, Unite and The Student Hotel are all actively investing in mainland Europe right now, which is a pretty solid tip that it's a wise move.

Silver

Silver is a tricky one because traders tend to be divided on its potential as an investment. It has been ranked among the safe havens over the years, but you need to stockpile a lot more silver than gold to hold the same amount of wealth. This has led to the metal being seen as gold's poor cousin. People who are trying to flog you the stuff are more likely to refer to it as 'the common man's gold'.

The second issue is that silver is crucial to many industrial processes, from medical applications to electronics, which means that it can be affected by economic slowdowns. While only 10–15% of the world's gold is used for jewellery or industry, it is estimated that half of all the silver produced is used in manufacturing.

Silver spikes in value during financial crises. If there were a money market meltdown and the government printed so much money that the pound became worthless, silver's popularity would soar, as would gold's. For example, during the 2008 recession, the price of silver doubled while the yellow metal's value rose 70%. But in the run-up to the 2016 referendum on the United Kingdom's membership in Europe, when the markets went haywire and the FTSE 100 lost £400 billion in four days, the price of gold rocketed from £824 to £920 an ounce. Silver rose too, but modestly, from £11 to £12.50 an ounce. Herein lies the problem with using historical performance to predict the future.

Silver has a reputation for rising in value much faster than gold in times of turmoil – but not always. It is generally a lot more volatile than gold, although it is still seen as a hedge against inflation.

How to invest in silver

For those of you expecting a financial apocalypse, I'm told that the best kind of silver to buy for bartering purposes in the ensuing Mad Max-esque world would be pre-1965 US 90% silver coins – also known as junk silver coins because they are valued on silver content alone, not as collectables – or 1 oz silver rounds. You may be better off with 1/10 oz Gold Eagles, 1/10 oz Krugerrands, 1/4 oz Gold Eagles or 1/4 oz Krugerrands, though.

It can be useful to compare the price of silver to that of gold to try to work out if either is overpriced. In June 2016, gold was almost 74 times more expensive than silver, which is higher than the average of 55. However, this has soared to 100 times on previous occasions and fallen to lows of 20 times.

If you are of the opinion that silver is under-priced and set to rise, you can invest through an ETF, or buy stocks in silver mines. Mining shares will tend to rise faster than commodity prices when in a bull market, but they can also fall much faster, too. You can buy silver bullion from the Royal Mint, or from brokers such as Coininvest and BullionByPost. The interesting thing about owning the physical metal is that it doesn't stop you from also shorting silver if you think the market is taking a tumble. Think of it as hedging.

An interesting niche in the silver market, and one that is getting a lot more attention lately, is antique silver. According to the art and antiques search engine Barneby's, antique silver objects such as candelabra, dinnerware, snuff boxes or ornamental silver are changing hands for significantly less than its smelted value. Put simply: it's under-priced.

Silver antiques are no longer fashionable – few people collect silver spoons or keep a silver tea service these days. And because it hasn't been in vogue for many years, a lot of the old silverware has been melted down and turned into bullion. It's possible that antique silver could make a comeback – stranger things have happened. If so, then items can be picked up cheaply now, ready for the market to turn. Barneby's research found that a Georgian silver coffee pot would have sold for £1,500 in the 1980s but now is worth between £800 and £1,000.

The company, which trawls listings of the biggest auction houses in the world, including Sotheby's and Christie's, recommends investing in items with unusual provenance. It points to a highly decorated soup tureen once owned by the sister of Queen Marie Antoinette, which sold for £447,000 at Bonhams on an estimate of £100,000 to £200,000. Pieces in Art Nouveau style have also been picked as winners by Barneby's.

LEGO®

Hoarders rejoice. LEGO sets have historically outperformed the FTSE 100 in the investment stakes. Since 2000, the sets – if in pristine condition – have increased in value by an average of 12% each year. This compares to a total rise of just 4.1% for the top UK listed companies – including dividends – during that time.

Canny investors don't have long to wait for the brightly coloured bricks to appreciate in value, as second-hand prices begin to rise as soon as the line is no longer in production. LEGO typically 'retires' sets after a couple of years – although there's no guarantee they won't resurrect them in future.

According to Ed Maciorowski, founder of LEGO investing site BrickPicker.com and author of *The Ultimate Guide to Collectible LEGO Sets*, this collectable has exploded with the growth of eBay. The worst-case scenario is that you can sell it for what you bought it for, he claims: 'Any high-end, larger set, anything that's popular, if you're willing to hang onto it for 10 years, it will appreciate to some degree. I haven't seen one yet that hasn't appreciated over that period.' If you're thinking back, in horror, to what your old 1980s LEGO Classic Space set would be worth now, stop torturing yourself. Newer sets – from the turn of this century – are proving more popular than retro ones, mainly because there are so few mint-condition, sealed box sets from 20–30 years ago that people don't know how to value them.

The business of investing in LEGO

How do you offload your LEGO set once it has appreciated in value? eBay is an option. Some modern sets that were released in 2014 sold for 36% more than their retail price in 2015 on the auction site, according to BrickPicker.com.

Ideally, you want to hang on to a set for a few years, however. 'Café Corner', a model hotel and café, went on sale for £89.99 in 2007. The LEGO set, which has more than 2,000 pieces, has seen its price sky-rocket to more than £2,000. According to LEGO marketplace Bricklink, even Café Corner sets that are used or unboxed can sell for up to £800, while some sets that are sealed are offered for £3,250.

The most popular type of LEGO set is *Star Wars* themed, accounting for 10 of the 20 most expensive sets currently being bought by enthusiasts. Beware of bulk buying every *Star Wars* set out there – many are reproduced over and over, driving down their value. Take the LEGO Death Star 10188. This has been reproduced every year for a decade or more.

There is also a danger that the fast-growing reseller community is actually skewing the market. They stockpile certain sets, which makes LEGO think there's a real market for them – but it's just investors bulk buying. Nonetheless, LEGO keeps producing the same set over and over to meet demand, driving down the value of the product.

Whichever sets you buy, try to keep these sets in pristine condition. Some sets that are opened, or worn, may still fetch a reasonable price if rare, and there are resellers who specialize in breaking up certain sets and selling them off piece by piece, generating a hefty profit – but for the amateur LEGO investor, it's probably a good idea to stick to the proven cash cows.

Mini-figures are also an interesting LEGO sub-class, and can be the driving force behind the set, making a humdrum scene much more valuable. Firestar Toys has a collectable mini-figures store online, and look out for kits with exclusive mini-figures, ideally with several included.

Building a LEGO investment is not without risk

There is always the danger with collectables that too many people will pile in and supply will outstrip demand. During 2015, the number of investors registered on BrickPicker.com rose from 39,000 to 50,000. Online learning platform Udemy even has a course in LEGO investing now, promising 39 hours of lectures.

But even if the UK and US markets reach saturation, the rise of new middle classes around the world will create opportunity for LEGO investment. 'LEGO is now hitting the Asian market', claims Maciorowski. 'There is a huge untapped Asian market out there, tonnes of people who will be wanting to buy, and will want the sets we're buying now.'

Arguably, the major winner from this trend is LEGO itself. In February 2015, the Danish company reported that sales had risen 15% to £2.8 billion, and profits had surged by 15%, too. Ten sets were sold every second during that year.

Which sets did the world's largest toymaker say outperformed the rest? Its city landmarks and *Star Wars* ranges were the bestsellers – investors' favourites, no less.

It's pretty easy to stay on top of new LEGO sets – there are umpteen toy blogs out there that announce new releases: Toysnbricks. com has a section dedicated to new and upcoming sets, for example.

There are other kinds of children's building block out there, but, for the moment, they aren't as collectable as LEGO. Could this change if rivals Meccano® or Mega Bloks® bring out a Hollywood box-office smash, like *The LEGO Movie*? Perhaps.

Diamonds

These may be a girl's best friend but they can be an investor's worst nightmare. Diamonds were almost consigned to the chapter on the 'ones that got away' because they are devilishly hard to value. But they remain a popular way for holding wealth, especially when gold loses its lustre, so are worth mentioning in a little detail.

Industry experts claim that polished diamonds have outperformed the FTSE 100 over the past decade, fuelled by demand from India and China. A recent report by De Beers, the diamond giant, shows that global diamond jewellery sales rose 3% in 2014, exceeding $80 billion for the first time. But in 2015 there was a softening in the market, according to the Diamond Price Statistics Annual Report published by Rapaport. It warned of sluggish consumer demand, and falling prices as manufacturers found themselves holding far more diamonds than they could sell. These stones traditionally sell well in China and Russia, but the recent anti-corruption campaign in China has resulted in a marked downturn in diamond purchases, and when the rouble plunged against the dollar and Russian oil prices took a dive, the Soviet elite's diamond fever cooled. This market is cyclical, and the big spenders will be back – this could be the best time to buy, when prices are low, in preparation for the next upturn.

How to invest in diamonds

There are a few different ways to invest in diamonds. The first is to actually buy the rocks themselves, which can be tempting, as they can be set into jewellery and worn. There are a few issues with owning physical diamonds: the first is where to buy them. If you buy a diamond from a jeweller, you will be forking out for a mark-up of 100% or more. This means you need to find a reputable trader, and try to get a wholesale price.

Diamonds are valued according to their shape, colour, size, cut, clarity, brilliance and imperfections (or lack of them) – hence why they are so tricky to price. Valuations are subjective, so one dealer's price may be different from another's – unlike commodities such as gold, which are fairly homogenous. According to Bain, the consultancy, there are a whopping 16,000 combinations that influence the price of each stone.

At least there is now a little more liquidity in this market. The Investment Diamond Exchange, based in Los Angeles, was launched in 2013, and is believed to be the first open diamond exchange. This means that private investors can buy and sell GIA-certified, investment-grade diamonds. The website claims that these gems are 'without inflated retail mark-up, with minimal fees and total transparency'. Literal transparency, as it happens – they only trade diamonds without colour.

It's worth paying particular attention to colour, however. 'Fancy colour' tends to add value. Almost all of the top 10 most expensive diamonds ever sold are categorized as 'fancy colour'. The rarest fancies are tinted red, green, purple and orange, but pink and blue are also highly prized. It's not really advisable to invest in a diamond worth less than £5,000.

Imagine you've snagged your purple diamond; there's now the small matter of storing and insuring it. You'll need tailored cover, and you don't want a burglar to make off with your carefully selected investment.

If you do decide to put a small percentage of your money in diamonds, and have a trusted dealer in your little black book, most experts recommend holding them for at least five years before selling on, in order to make a return. The Rapaport Diamond Trade Index, an industry benchmark, shows that three-carat diamonds increased in value by 145% between 1999 and 2011, while five-carat diamonds increased in value by 171%.

The price growth shows no sign of slowing, especially at the top end. In May 2016, the Unique Pink diamond ring was sold at a Sotheby's auction for £21.6 million, and Christie's auctioned the Oppenheimer Blue for a record-breaking £39.8 million.

You don't have to actually own the gems; you can invest in diamond mine shares or buy into a diamond fund. There are dedicated commodities funds with some precious stones in the mix; these can be accessed most easily through an ETF – we met this beast in Chapter 2.

If you're thinking about investing in diamond mines, however, a note of caution. Economic volatility can affect mining companies very quickly, as it's an expensive and challenging business getting these gems out of the earth. Take a quick look at the diamond miners listed on Miningfeeds.com/diamonds-mining-report-all-countries and check out how many share prices are in the red, and how many green. At the time of writing, losers to winners stood at 9:4. Five miners showed no movement in their share price. In 2016, Russia's Vladimir Putin put a chunk of Alrosa, the world's biggest miner of diamonds, on sale to encourage investors to send some capital his way. Just under half of Alrosa is owned by the Russian state.

The allure of diamonds

But let's take a minute to understand why diamonds are valuable. Humans can now make perfect and beautiful synthetic diamonds, which rival those made by nature. These hunks of carbon are extremely useful for all kinds of manufacturing processes – cutting, for example, but they only really became highly prized in the mid-1900s, after De Beers launched a marketing campaign, creating the cult of the diamond engagement ring; before the Second World War, only 10% of engagement rings contained diamonds.

At this time, the world was swamped with diamonds, so many that their value should have plunged. So De Beers constrained supply, told ordinary people they were a luxury, and the rest is history.

I like to think that, one day, the price of diamonds will reflect their abundance, and you'll find them in vending machines for a fiver. In this imaginary universe, genuinely rare gemstones will become sought after for jewellery, such as colour-changing alexandrite, which is currently $12,000 per carat, and tanzanite, which is 1,000 times rarer than diamond.

Buy-to-let

The buy-to-let market has suffered blow after blow, after the government and the UK's high street banks raised the bar for buying property and made it much harder to make a living out of it.

From April 2016, second-home buyers and buy-to-let investors were required to pay a higher rate of stamp duty when buying a property. This is a 3% surcharge, which sits on top of the rate for the value of the property they are buying. In past years, properties worth between £40,000 and £125,000 were exempt from stamp duty, but they are now subject to it. Properties worth less than £40,000 are still exempt, but good luck with finding a great buy-to-let investment for less than £40,000.

To make life more difficult for the buy-to-let landlord, several lenders have also tightened their qualifying criteria for buy-to-let mortgages, such as raising their minimum rental cover, which is the amount by which rental payments exceed mortgage costs. They are demanding much higher deposits, too – as much as 40%. Around half of buy-to-let mortgages sold previously required only a 25% deposit, according to figures from the broker Mortgages for Business. Mortgage charges tend to be much higher in buy-to-let compared to buying a home.

The last piece of the puzzle will fall into place come 2021, when landlords will no longer be able to deduct the cost of their mortgage interest from their rental income when they calculate the tax due. Instead of taking the mortgage cost out to work out the profit, this will be replaced with a tax credit equal to 20% of the total taxable income. This change is set to be phased in over a four-year period from April 2017.

This effectively means that landlords are paying tax on their entire income from the buy-to-let property, so they are taxed on turnover, not profit. This could make some of these investments loss-making. Here's an example. Imagine that you're a 40% taxpayer, your buy-to-let is making £20,000 a year and the mortgage repayments for that period total £13,000. At the moment, you pay tax on the £7,000 difference – that is, the profit, meaning that £2,800 goes to the taxman and you keep the balance. From 2020, you'll pay 40% tax on the £20,000, with a 20% tax credit. This means the taxman gets £5,400, so your bill will have gone up 93%. You, as the landlord, get only £1,600. Landlords are trying to figure out ways around this. One option is to become a company, and pay Corporation Tax on profits instead of this new tax. This is not straightforward, however. You have to prove that this is a business, and that you, the landlord, take care of the day-to-day maintenance and management of tenants. If you employ a middleman to take care of these things or have a separate full-time job, the property is likely to be classed as an investment and not a company. Mortgage rates also tend to be a little higher for businesses, and you'll have to complete annual returns and file them with Companies House.

London has lost its lustre

If you are still keen to invest in buy-to-let, the experts warn that London may not be the best place to buy. Property values have exploded in recent years, and rents have not quite kept pace, meaning that you're stumping up a lot of cash that won't be easily realized in rental yields. Those chasing strong yields are looking to places outside the capital, typically areas where property has previously been neglected, but where there have been corporate relocations, a significant increase in inward investment, and where property prices have not kept up with the rest of the UK. Basically, you want to focus on an area where there is no shortage of tenants. According to Garrington Property Finders, the company set up by Phil Spencer, the TV presenter from *Location, Location, Location*, property prices and rent are rising the most strongly in Manchester, with prices set to rise 24% and rents 23% by 2020. Property is still cheap, relative to London, with target lot sizes ranging from £150,000 to £250,000.

Another hotspot for buy-to-let is Cambridge, which is looking attractive because of the successful industry cluster based there. It is home to a number of companies that trade globally, and so are not held hostage by sterling crises or problems in Europe.

Investors seeking to pile into buy-to-let property are advised to go for freeholds over leaseholds, and houses tend to be a better bet than a single flat in an apartment block. This is because your investment will compete with all the other flats in the block, which will probably look very similar, meaning that the only way to compete is on price. Experts recommend investing in either new-builds – or almost new – or Victorian properties in good shape, with a full record of recent works to prove that the wiring is sound, and so on. The highest yields are to be found in HMO properties, driven by a new trend whereby young professionals prefer to live in house-shares with likeminded people instead of owning a home.

When becoming a buy-to-let landlord, your obligations don't end once you have placed a tenant in your property. The onus is on you to maintain that property, and the rules have been tweaked to make it your responsibility to check things such as Right to Rent – is your tenant legally allowed to be in the UK? There are health and safety considerations, and complaints could take up a lot of your time. Go into the buy-to-let business with your eyes open.

Forestry

The UK forestry market has become an interesting investment niche in recent years. It's attractive because investors benefit from income generated from commercial timber production, alongside the increase in capital worth from the appreciation of the land itself.

According to research by Savills and Scottish Woodlands, the value of this market has increased by more than 200% over the past five years. The average value per productive hectare – forest that's being cut down and replanted – rose by 13.5% during 2015 to £8,615 per hectare. This has prompted many investors to pile in, and £137 million was ploughed into the UK forestry market in 2015.

Forests do not come cheap, and investment minimums stand at several hundred thousands of pounds. There are some collective investments that allow investors to put a smaller amount of money into a central pot for a share in a forest, but insiders say these generate little value. Generally speaking, you want to have the biggest forest you can to make it worth your while.

One of the greatest benefits of investing in forest is that it's 'tax benign'. A few years ago, timber was taken out of the tax system because the government wanted to incentivize people to grow it. This is a super-long-term crop; no one in the UK would bother with it if it proved expensive as well as time-consuming.

If you fell timber, the income from that is not taxable. We're not talking about tax reliefs here, it's actually tax-free. If you buy a forest and then sell it again, the Capital Gains Tax (CGT) calculation is based solely on the land value, not the timber, because it's classed as a crop. Forests have also proved a handy way to bring down Inheritance Tax bills, as they are eligible for business property relief after two years, which means no death tax.

See the wood for the trees

The location of the site will have a huge impact on its value. The best investments in recent years have been in the south of Scotland and the Borders, although prices are now rising in England and Wales because there is a scarcity of forest available. The site must be easy to access from main roads to speed up the process of getting the timber from source to customer – ideally you want to be located as close to your target market as possible, as wood is expensive to transport.

The quality of the land is important; the better it is, the faster your forest will grow. The age and species of the forest are also key: commercial spruce forests that are well established are more attractive than younger forests with different species, such as conifer. Sitka and Norway Spruce are the favoured species. However, the long-term investor, with a 10- or even 20-year outlook, may find that newer plantations prove lucrative down the line. It's worth noting that it takes between 35 and 55 years for the spruce to reach maturity.

Market drivers

There is likely to be demand for wood for many years to come. There has been an upturn in the use of wood for domestic construction in recent years, and an explosion in the use of biomass – wood that is ground up and burnt to produce heat and electricity. The weakening of sterling has also made domestically produced timber more attractive to UK companies. This country imports a lot of timber, and a weak pound means that these imports are more expensive, so it's better to source from home.

But investors looking at this asset class should not pay too close attention to short-term market movements. Experts advise holding on to forests for a minimum of 10 years, and ideally as long as possible. In many cases, the patient investor will make more out of the rising value of the asset than from the sale of timber during that time – although not always.

Never forget that this is an entirely illiquid asset, but one with a fairly predictable and steady growth pattern, and that's what you're relying on to make you a return.

Wine

The world's wealthy oenophiles have long invested in fine wines; an estimated one-quarter of high-net-worth individuals around the world currently own a wine collection, which on average represents 2% of their wealth.

Why is wine so popular? Put bluntly, even if it all goes wrong you can still drink the assets.

Joking aside, investing in fine wine is big business these days. The growing numbers of wine-focused funds, which specialize in trading high-end grape juice, have even attracted big money from institutional investors – pension funds, banks and insurance companies. This is quite the vote of confidence for fine wine.

Wine is an interesting asset in that it performs differently from equities or oil, so is a useful balance for a portfolio. Advisers usually recommend putting no more than 10% of your pot into wine, but it's a handy diversifier.

The Wine Investment Fund (WIF), which specializes in buying and trading the top wines of the Bordeaux region in France, is one of the more established wine funds, paying out an average of 7.2% in returns to its investors in the 12 years since its 2003 launch. It charges 20% of any profit that it makes, so is incentivized to work for the highest possible returns, and will only look at wines costing £500 a case or more.

Not all wines make good investments

Investors could learn quite a lot from the WIF's rules of engagement; it won't look at '*en primeur*' wines – those that are still in the barrel. Why? Because earlier in life, wine prices are far more volatile. Also, '*en primeur*' investing became so popular in 2009 and 2010 that some of those wines are actually cheaper now than when they were released. Five to 25 years old is the sweet spot for this fund.

Why only Bordeaux? Because wines from Bordeaux tend to have a longer lifespan – drinkable up to 50 years after bottling if stored properly.

Bordeaux is also a clearly defined region – measuring precisely 49.36 km^2 – which means the chances of thousands of new vines suddenly appearing in the area are slim. This is an issue in other wine-making regions, such as the New World, where vineyards can spring up suddenly, flooding the market with new wine and driving down prices.

Research by Elroy Dimson, Peter Rousseau and Christophe Spaenjers for an article published a few years back entitled 'The Price of Wine' found that Bordeaux premier crus have beaten bonds, gold and art in terms of real financial returns over the long term. Using data from 1900 to 2012, they showed that the net gains, when transaction fees and the cost of storing the wine were stripped out, hit 4.1%, which was beaten only by equities, which generated returns of 5% in that time.

The limited supply of Bordeaux wine means that as time passes – and bottles of the stuff are consumed – logic dictates that the dwindling supply will increase in value. The same is true of Burgundy wines, which are also arguably a smart investment. Fine wine investment company Cult Wines reckons that over the past decade an investment in Burgundy would have yielded a compounded annual return of 10.63%.

Large funds are less keen on the Burgundy region, however, because production is almost too small to make it worth their while.

How to invest in wine

You want to focus on a wine that is frequently traded because that creates market liquidity – pardon the pun. Simply put, you want an investment that is easy to get out of because other people want to buy it, not one that you're stuck with against your will.

One important lesson that a first-time wine investor must learn, according to William Grey, WIF's investment manager, is that personal taste must play no part in which wines you back. If you go to dinner and find a certain vintage fabulously quaffable, that makes no difference to whether it's a strong buy or sell.

There is one man whose opinion does count, however. That man is Robert Parker, a US wine critic and the 'guru' of wine ratings. The Maryland-born market mover is famed for his use of a 100-point scoring system, which can all be found online and has been known to make – or break – a producer's fortune.

For top Bordeaux wines, 'Parker Points' are crucial indicators of value, and the difference between a 99-pointer and a 100-pointer can be hundreds or even thousands of pounds. In 2015, Parker announced that he was passing his mantle to an Englishman, Neal Martin, who will now be tasting wines '*en primeur*', but his Parker Points live on.

Investors can find out the live prices of different wines by using Liv-ex, which is like the London Stock Exchange but for wine. Ordinary people can't actually trade on there – it's only for merchants – but you can check out the data, read the blogs on the site and generally educate yourself about the big movers and shakers in the wine market. Liv-ex is a useful resource because it's independent, and based on actual trades, or – where there's a dearth of data – on the spread between the bid and the offer. If you decide to work with a wine fund, it's worth asking how they come up with valuations. If it's all done through some black-box process, in-house, beware. Funds have become unstuck in the past because they valued wines themselves, or used a friendly merchant, who happened to have a lot of a certain wine in stock and wanted to line his pocket.

Could wine investing leave you with a nasty hangover?

Fine wine investment has hit the headlines for all the wrong reasons in recent years. If you are investing in wine, you want that wine to be held in a UK government bonded warehouse. You should be able to physically visit the wine, if required, and any company that says that is impossible should be avoided. Be wary of funds that cold call you, or send unsolicited mail, and check that they have a real office, not a virtual or serviced address – as with the wine, visit the office, if you can. Always ask about insurance – if a warehouse full of your wine burns to the ground, you want to receive the value of the wine at the time of the accident – which should actually be higher than the price you paid, because the asset will appreciate.

Fine wine, as an asset class, has had a bumpy few years. It generated its third year of negative returns in 2015, owing to waning Asian demand and some poor vintage years for Bordeaux. Here's why this doesn't mean that wine is a bad investment. The global economy is perking up again: wine-guzzling markets such as Japan, where consumption dropped off sharply following the 2011 earthquake and tsunami, are buying again. The crackdown on gift-giving in China – the government has been trying to eradicate corporate bribery disguised as bottles of Chateau Lafite – is now being offset by a rising, and sophisticated, middle class that wants ever-finer wines. Cult Wines recently claimed that of the US$352 million in wine sold at auction in 2014, some US$104 million – 30% – was bought by Hong Kong alone. By 2024 it is predicted that China will boast nearly

15,700 ultra-high-net-worth individuals and 338 billionaires; the nation's consumption of wine has been growing by 20% a year.

Nevertheless, the value of the overall wine market dropped 9% in 2014, according to wine business Berry Bros & Rudd. Over the long term, however, the patient investor will see gains. From 2005 to 2014, the market grew by 134%. Investors also pay no duty or VAT on wine when it's 'under bond' – not being drunk. Also, because wine eventually goes bad, it's classed as a 'wasting asset', which means you won't pay any CGT.

Whisky

A new stock market for whisky launched in 2015, which allows investors to trade whisky in a similar way to wine for the first time. WhiskyDirectInvest has turned whisky into a new asset class at a time when the global demand for rare whisky is rising steeply. According to consultancy Rare Whisky 101, the value of bottles of rare Scotch whisky rose 12.57% over the year to December 2015, and is up more than 200% since 2008.

At the moment, WhiskyInvestDirect is entirely focused on Scotch whiskies – this is for a variety of reasons. One is that founder Rupert Patrick, who has worked at drinks giant Diageo, and whisky brands Jim Beam and Macleod Distillers, is an expert in Scotch whiskies and has relationships with many of the big distilleries in Scotland.

Another is that Scottish distilleries hold an average of nine years' worth of stock at any one time, because this whisky is matured slowly – all Scotch whisky must be aged in oak barrels for at least three years to even be called Scotch. This is a huge burden on the 115 distilleries licensed to produce the stuff, which can't make money on their product for several long, expensive years. There are currently some 20 million casks lying maturing in warehouses in Scotland.

This is no doubt why the distillers agreed to do a deal with WhiskyInvestDirect to sell some of their new spirit – Scotch before it can be called Scotch – to the platform to be traded.

This new whisky is an interesting asset, because investors get into the market when the spirit is at its cheapest – no mark-up or margin has been built in, and there's no tax to pay on it yet. In technical terms, it's an 'uninflated asset'. The one cost that you do pay is WhiskyInvestDirect's commission – 1.75% at present – and its storage charge, which is more expensive at 5.45%. The whisky is held in bonded warehouses, and insured, so that investors receive the full value of the whisky if anything happens to it, which will be greater than the price paid for it because the stuff appreciates so quickly.

Once the storage cost is factored in, the return for investors so far has been 9% before inflation, so a real return of 7%, and investors can pile in from as little as £2 per litre, wholesale. There is no minimum investment, and investors aren't forced to hold on to the whisky for any set period of time.

Other ways to invest in whisky

There is another option for fans of the dram: the world's first whisky fund launched last year in Hong Kong (2015). The Platinum Whisky Investment Fund is for high rollers only, with a minimum stake of $250,000, and investors are not covered by the UK's Financial Services Compensation Scheme (FSCS).

Playing the whisky stock market is far more accessible than attempting to get involved in buying and selling rare whiskies at the top end of the market. To give you an idea of the money changing hands, the most expensive whisky ever sold at auction is the six-litre Macallan M Decanter-Constantine, which was bought from Sotheby's in Hong Kong in January 2014 for an eye-watering $628,000 (£380,168). But those who are keen to bid for top whiskies should head to Bonhams, which holds four dedicated whisky auctions each year. Be aware that auction houses will charge up to 25% of the value of whiskies in return for selling them, although online auctions may be cheaper.

Fine whiskies tend to follow a similar growth trajectory to the global economy. When people feel that they have more cash in their pocket, they buy a more expensive whisky. Evidence shows that Scotch remains an aspirational spirit in many global markets.

There has been a slowdown in Scotch whisky sales in recent years, especially in Europe, which suffered during the last recession, but pundits claim that 2016 will see a resurgence of the 'water of life', especially in emerging markets in South America, where the middle classes are flourishing.

That said, not all whiskies will appreciate in value, which is why it's extremely important to have a diversified portfolio. In 2015, for example, the worst-performing 100 bottles in the Rare Whisky 101 index lost almost 7% of their value over a six-month period. The best-performing 100 bottles gained 8.93%, however, with stand-outs including Bowmore and Glenfiddich.

As with wine, whisky is currently classed as a 'wasting asset', which means that CGT doesn't have to be paid on your investment profits.

Conclusion

Learning about risky investments is a useful way to test out your risk appetite. Once the risks are explained and the returns set out clearly, you can make an informed decision. For example, does investing in the new whisky stock market seem attractive, even though you know that the idea of it is very new and untested? Does it make you curious about riskier investments?

The danger lies in the fact that high-risk investments are usually much more exciting than the safe ones. A smart investor must not have their head turned by a sexy story. Ask yourself: how do the options outlined fit in with my plan? Is the final figure I want to reach at the front of my mind?

You need to bring yourself back to that original plan as frequently as possible: are you saving for a deposit? Trying to put together a healthy retirement fund? Think of that dream as grandma's house, and you are Little Red Riding Hood. Can you follow the path safely to her door, or will the big bad wolf of high-risk investing lead you astray?

High-risk investments can bring significant returns, but make sure you have the basics right before you start adding these elements to the mix.

The closer you are to your target figure, the less risk you should take. You don't want to suddenly lose a massive chunk of your pot because of a reckless investment at the eleventh hour. If your portfolio is falling short of your target, however, it may be time to assume a little more risk.

Risky

04

The investments in this chapter have been classified as risky, either because the margin for error is very high or there is a reasonable risk you could lose your money. This doesn't mean that these aren't bets worth making, but certainly not on a whim, and only a very small proportion of your investable assets.

If investors want higher potential returns, they have to be willing to take on higher risk. If anyone tries to peddle a low-risk investment that apparently promises market-beating returns, it's probably a scam.

You need to work out what level of risk you're ready to accept. Strategies for doing this vary, but a good starting point is to look up your timeline and the amount of money you can afford to lose. The timeline is important, because the longer you have to invest, the more time you have to recoup any losses that happen in the short term. If you have £25,000 to invest but you will need it in a year's time to put a deposit down on a flat, you don't want to go for high-risk investment options. You may be forced to sell when prices are low because you can't wait any longer. The longer you have, the less likelihood of being forced to sell out at cut-rate prices.

As for how much you can afford to lose, this may seem a bit pessimistic but it is important to understand the implications of losing all the money you invest; what are you putting on the line? Only invest the amount of money that you can afford to lose or, at the very least, the amount that you are happy to tie up for a period of time. The wealthier you are, the more risk you are usually able to take, because you are less affected by losses. If you have only £5,000 to your name, and you lose it all, you're going to be in a significantly worse financial position than a millionaire who loses £5,000.

Foreign currency trading (forex)

The act of changing one currency into another – foreign exchange – has become an industry in its own right, with traders attempting to make a living betting on price movements. There are a few ways to do this. One is by taking advantage of favourable interest rates. Say the interest rate in the UK is about to be stripped down to 0%, but the Federal Reserve is about to raise interest rates in the United States to 1%. You could try to take advantage of the stronger rate by selling pounds and buying dollars. Then, once your account is full of greenbacks, leave it there for a while to enjoy the 1% rate.

The other way to make money is to try to predict currency movements based on the performance of a country's economy. If you believe that sterling is going to depreciate against the dollar, you could buy dollars, wait for sterling to fall as expected, then switch your dollars back into sterling and make a profit. Many traders did just this when the UK was poised to vote on leaving the European Union. Before the referendum result, the pound was at £1.50 to the dollar, so those expecting it to fall bought dollars. The day after the Leave vote was announced, it fell to £1.34, and they switched back, making a reasonable profit.

How currency trading works

In currency trading you are always comparing one currency to another, so forex is always quoted in pairs.

Let's take a minute to explain the standard quote screen, which can appear confusing. Quotes show the base currency first – the domestic currency, say – and this will always be in a denomination of 1. The counter currency comes second – so it costs x amount of the counter currency to buy one of the base currency.

The quote will show two prices: the buy and the sell. These are the prices that the forex market maker is willing to buy or sell at. The difference between the two prices is the spread: the buy:sell spread in forex is similar to the bid:ask spread in equities trading.

The reason why the spread is important is that this helps you to work out the risk involved at the point of trade. The spread is like the commission you pay to trade.

Forex prices are always quoted to four decimal places, which is important because you may hear the word 'pip', which describes the tiny price movements. The pip is the impact of that last decimal place. From 1.1200 to 1.1205 is five pips. You multiply the number of pips by the amount you want to move from one currency into another to work out the price of the risk involved.

Traders work to different timelines – some are day traders, who love watching their screens all day and moving money around constantly to make tiny gains. This is highly speculative – and can be a full-time job. You're constantly looking for hints that economies might outperform or underperform other economies, so you'll become obsessed with speeches from the Bank of England Governor and data from the Office for National Statistics. Others will just wait for obvious opportunities to come up a few times a year.

The gains you make from currency trading are taxable like other income, but this is why some traders prefer to bet on movements using tax-free options such as spread betting or contracts for difference – more on these later – which are basically just gambling.

Can you make money?

The answer is yes, but it's risky. Currencies may never recover against other nations' money. Look at the dollar to the pound: eight years ago you could get $2 for every £1. The pound hasn't even approached that level since. And it's hard to make a lot of money without betting a lot of cash. Insiders tell me that some beginners have lofty ideas about turning £5,000 into £40,000 in a year, but that's almost never possible. Really good traders can make annual returns of between 50% and 100% – but that's if they are super lucky/talented/psychic – delete where applicable.

The reason why many people get into this market is that the cost of trading is now pretty low – often cheaper than trading shares. There's so much liquidity in forex, with $5 trillion moving between currencies each day, and a lot of competition, forcing spreads to narrow as banks and other institutions battle for your business. Spreads can be as low as 1.5 pips for big transactions these days, compared to as many as 5 a few years back.

You will be wrong as often as you are right

This can be a strange thing to get your head around, but forex traders are wrong about half the time. This doesn't mean they don't make money, however. They end up in profit because of strict money and risk management. You want your trades to have a good 'risk to reward ratio'. Say you were going to risk £500 on a trade – how much would you make if it works out? Is it £1,000 or £750? You always want to know what you stand to gain as well as lose, and make the trades with the healthiest returns – don't bet your money on tiny gains. If you get the risk to reward ratio right, you can afford to be wrong 50% of the time and still make money.

The one benefit that small, independent traders have over big funds is that they can move much faster. Some hedge funds have to spend a long time building a position. They are so huge that they could actually move the market by selling or buying huge tranches of a specific currency. They are the tankers in the market; small traders are the speed boats. They can change position quickly, jumping in and out on small opportunities.

Futures and options

There are many different kinds of derivatives out there, but, according to traders, futures and options – or 'F&O' to those in the know – are the least dangerous kind. These are a kind of speculation on a future price move; a bet on where a market will go. Importantly, they are tied to the performance of an underlying asset, such as shares or commodities.

These tend to be bets on globally recognized exchanges, which means that the information about price movement is publicly available and easy to access. If it is not based on this kind of underlying asset, don't touch it.

Unlike spread betting, where your losses can vastly exceed your deposits, your liability with options is limited – if you make a £5,000 speculation and you lose that, that's all you're going to lose on that deal. You pay the margin on the trade, and you're in. This differs from more complex derivatives, where you may assume there's a fixed liability but actually you can be stung for more money if the market goes against you. Futures too can cost you more money than you stumped up initially.

The other difference between options and futures is this: an option is a contract that sets the price that you can either buy or sell a certain stock for at a subsequent time – but you are not obliged to buy or sell. A future – or futures contract – is a contract to sell or buy a commodity at a later date, at a price agreed upon in advance – and you do have to buy or sell.

The standard time frame is three months, although it can be more, and there are four time frames to bet on each year. These are March, June, September and December. Say you're reading this in December 2016, you could then bet to March, or even December 2017 if you're looking for a longer-term play. Most trading happens in September – stock markets tend to be a little more sluggish in summer and at Christmas time.

There are some important differences between American and European options. One example of a fundamental difference is that owners of an American-style option can exercise that option at any point until the option's expiry date. With a European option, you can only exercise it on the actual expiration date.

American and European options also stop trading at different times: American options cease trading at the close of play on the third Friday of the month. European options stop trading the day before.

Futures and options are a form of insurance and are used by businesses to hedge their bets – when dealing in foreign currency, for example.

How to trade F&O

Hopefully, you're still with me, because there are a few more terms to explain. When dealing with these kinds of second-level securities, you need to understand call and put options, fancy lingo for buying and selling. A call option gives the investor the right, but not the obligation, to purchase a stock, or commodity or financial instrument, at a specified price at or before a specified date. A put option does the same thing, but gives the investor the right to sell.

To make this even more complicated, a call option will have a buyer and a seller, who will want the underlying asset to do polar opposite things. The buyer of a call option will profit when the price of the underlying shares goes up, but the seller – or the 'writer' of the call option – will make their money only if the underlying shares decline. Similarly, with put options, the buyer profits if the shares fall in value while the writer really wants the price to rise.

I like to imagine the writers hopping up and down on the spot, hoping that options expire before the underlying stock rises or falls in value. If your call fails, your bet has backfired and you've lost your money. But, if the underlying asset that your put is based on rises in value instead of falls, you don't have to exercise your option. You may still come out on top because of the increase in value generated by the option, hopefully more than the price of the put.

Unlike options, which don't bind the investor to actually buying or selling the thing, a future is a legally binding contract to sell or buy the underlying commodity, regardless of whether you want to by that time or not.

A brief history of futures

How did all this financial tomfoolery come about? Futures trading was spawned by the agricultural sector, by farmers who wanted to secure their financial futures. Fearing a glut of wheat at harvest time, which would drive down the price of their crop, they would make a deal with a broker to sell the lot for a set price. The price might be below the current market rate, but could be much higher than the price a few months down the line, if the bottom drops out of the market. Farmers typically settled on a tiny margin above the costs of actually growing the stuff, so that they wouldn't go bankrupt if everything went to hell. The broker, on the other hand, hoped that there would be a wheat shortage and that the crop would actually be worth many times the cost of the futures contract, and the farmer would have to take pennies while the broker sold on the grain for a song. Modern-day investors, like those farmers, are transferring risk to the broker, but the wheat has been replaced by financial instruments – ones and zeros.

Trading futures is not for beginners. Newcomers to investing are far better off trading index trackers or exchange-traded funds. The one benefit that F&O gives the investor is that it allows you to put down a fraction of the amount it would cost you to buy the shares, yet enjoy (or suffer) the same exposure. They are attractive to those looking for whopping great leverage. Say you're keen to invest now but you want to use the money that you've made selling your house. Using a leveraged product like futures, you don't have to wait until the cash is cleared. That said, private investors rarely play in this end of the park. Hedge funds, pensions funds, these are the typical investors seeking out this level of leverage.

One reason why a private investor may want to look at futures is if they have a hunch that several market trends will take place at once. For example, they may believe that the FTSE will rise and the DAX – the German stock exchange – will fall. Futures allows you to place concurrent bets over a specific time frame. Tips for small investors dabbling in futures include: withdraw excess funds each month so you're not tempted to send good money after bad; try to maintain a 1:3 risk and reward ratio. You don't want to be betting £100 to make £25.

Classic cars

Classic cars are the ultimate passion or hobby investment. For more than 100 years, the super-rich have bought high-end motors as a way to show off their wealth and status, and the pastime is as popular today as it has ever been. The definition of a classic car varies widely, but it is generally accepted that cars made between 1950 and 1975 fall into this bracket. The whole category is extremely subjective, as much depends on the age of the collector. Ask a 65-year-old to say what 'classic car' means to them, and they're likely to point to those from the late 1950s, early 1960s; the cars they aspired to own when they were young. Ask people in their thirties, and their idea of classic may be a car from the mid-1980s. That said, any car that is 25 years old or more is road tax exempt, which is a sort of rolling classification for these types of vintage motor.

The classic car market, like many passion investments, is extremely opaque. Collectors tend to form networks, trading their cars privately, which means there is very little data on price points, what drives the market, or which cars are likely to appreciate in value. The market is also extremely illiquid. You can't get out of your investment, at the price you think is fair, whenever you want to – you have to find a buyer, and the car will only be worth what he or she is willing to pay for it.

Then there's the insurance issue. Unlike most of the investments that you may need to insure, working out how much to insure your classic car for is a palaver. Insurance values are based on the cost to replace the original, and classic cars are irreplaceable – a new one would be worth significantly less and it may be impossible to find a similar one from the same era with the same provenance and so on. Specialist insurers will work with collectors to come up with an agreed value – if it's stolen, this is the amount that will be paid out. Your premiums will be based on that assumption, so if the insurer thinks your 1960s Mini is worth £10,000 but you say it's actually closer to £20,000 because of its sentimental value or any other reason, remember you'll pay through the nose if you get your target valuation.

At least investors don't have to pay any Capital Gains Tax on their classic cars. They are seen as 'depreciating assets', even if their value goes up and not down with time.

The Ferrari effect

Given that it's incredibly difficult to find a particular car and put a price to it, experts warn that classic cars should not be seen as a pure investment and must not be compared to other traditional products, such as bonds and equities. Collecting these beauties should be seen as a bit of fun, with a kicker. That said, we do know that one brand of car has consistently outperformed all the other marques over the past 20 years – and that's Ferrari.

Some of the most valuable cars in the world today are collectable Ferraris from the fifties and sixties. The most valuable ones usually have three things in common: they have racing pedigrees and were often raced in one of the great competitions of their time; we know who owned it, and have evidence that such-and-such celebrity or famous racer has sat in the driver's seat; and it has an unblemished record – it was never involved in an accident. These three things have helped the top few cars pull away from the average in terms of value. Why Ferrari? It's the one brand that has always been in Formula One. Others, such as Aston Martin, have dipped in and out over the years. Ferrari's entire pedigree is around racing, and the marque has won the most championships out of any constructor. Ferrari also has a great reputation for its road cars, and production of these vehicles has been limited; you don't see them rolling off factory lines in their multiple millions, like cars from Toyota or General Motors.

One of the most coveted Ferraris is the 1964 Ferrari 250 GTO. One of these can trade in the tens of millions, as there are only 35 of them in the world – in 2013, a 250 GTO sold for more than $38 million. Other cars that consistently do well are: the British E-type Jaguar and any Aston Martin that has been featured in a James Bond film. The one thing that has really helped the market in recent years is the rise of the internet and the ability to send cars all over the world. Wealthy collectors in Japan can now find the car they desire in Rome online and can have it in their garage within weeks.

Among the rising stars, however, are eighties motors, which are proving popular with younger high-net-worth investors. Hot tips include the BMW M3, the Ford Escort RS Turbo and a Ford Sierra Cosworth RS500, which have seen prices soar. If you're trying to buy a modern classic, with the expectation that it will go up in value – and this is gigantic risk – focus on cars that have limited production runs and cult appeal.

Driving strong returns

One of the rare indices that attempt to monitor the market is the Knight Frank Luxury Index. Its most recent bit of digging found that classic car values have soared by 487% since 2006. The best brands returned 16% to investors last year (2015), based on data from the Historic Automobile Group International, which holds data on the top 50 collectable cars in the world. Note the fact that the figures only take into account the 'top 50', not the market as a whole. It's like telling you the fat content of milk but only looking at the cream on top.

Never forget that investing in a single car is a big gamble, just like buying a single stock. Some experts have warned that the inflated valuations may point to a bubble – and bubbles tend to burst quite dramatically when you least expect it. In the late eighties, early nineties, when classic cars were last at their zenith, many speculators who bought old motors – often highly leveraged deals, too – were caught with their pants down when the market stalled suddenly. There is also a huge problem with fakes and replicas. Ferrari, for example, has a whole department dedicated to finding these copies: no one wants to end up with a fake 250 GTO.

Another point to add is that we don't know what the advent of driverless cars may do to the market. Will future drivers yearn for the old models, or will humanity move wholesale into a driverless universe, making classic cars entirely redundant, like VHS tapes or minidiscs? Experts simply don't know, but it is believed that rare classic cars will always have cachet. 'They give bragging rights: you own something no one else has', one dealer told me. 'As long as you have wealthy people, and they have hobbies, classic cars will have their place.'

You don't have to buy the physical car to get involved in this market. Indeed, those who do buy tend to go for fixer-uppers, and invest many tens of thousands in restoration and storage, which is not to everyone's taste. Instead, you can buy into a classic car fund. These are very opaque and hard to track down – most are also offshore. One such fund is the Classic Car Fund, which both buys and sells top models and invests in car manufacturer shares. The minimum investment for this fund is £145,000, and it charges an annual management fee of 1.5% alongside a one-off 5% charge upon joining. It claims returns of more than 7%, but as it is domiciled in St. Vincent and the Grenadines, investors' cash is not covered by the Financial Conduct Authority's regulatory regime.

Stamps

Stamp collecting was still all the rage in the eighties when I was a child – I had a rather pathetic scrap book of them, which was lost long ago – but the hobby has been steadily falling out of fashion over the past century, with the number of stamp collectors worldwide dropping from around 200 million a few decades ago to 60 million in 2013, according to *The Wall Street Journal*.

That said, stamp investing is still big business, driven by an unprecedented explosion of interest from Asia; 40 million of the 60 million collectors hail from Asia, and 20 million of those from China alone. The rising Asian middle classes have become attached to these miniature works of art, with their unique designs and often historical or cultural significance.

China's stamp market is arguably the most dynamic in the world right now. In 1989, it was worth just $550,500. By 2012, it had ballooned into a $6,911,100 mega-market. Chinese enthusiasts were only allowed to start collecting stamps 40 years ago, following the death of the former premier, Chairman Mao, who saw the hobby as too decadent. If you stumble upon any old Chinese stamps from the late 19th or early 20th centuries at a car boot sale, snap them up quickly.

The Penny Black

The Penny Black is the world's oldest stamp and was launched in 1840, featuring a profile of Queen Victoria. Costing just a penny at the time, one very rare Penny Black on a postal notice is currently listed for sale as part of a 'prestige collection' on the website of Stanley Gibbons, the world's largest stamp merchant, for £150,000.

Stanley Gibbons has its own index, the GB250 Index, which launched just over a decade ago and is listed on Bloomberg. The index tracks the performance of the top 250 traded stamps from Great Britain. The index has actually never fallen, showing a compound annual growth rate of 11.96% between 2004 and 2014.

The GB30 Rarities Index, which features the 30 most desirable classic British postage stamps, has generated a compound annual growth rate of more than 10% per annum for the last 40 years.

The Stanley Gibbons website makes a bold claim about stamp investing: 'Investment grade stamps have consistently grown in value since records began', it says. 'During the 2008 financial crash their value rose 38.6%, as per the GB30 Index and 32% according to the GB250. Governments can print more money. Miners can mine more gold or diamonds, but nobody can print more Penny Blacks.'

Of course, the price stated by Stanley Gibbons is only a guide to the value of the stamp – the actual amount is determined according to collectors' demand. A Stanley Gibbon's spokeswoman has noted that it's a common fallacy that a price in their catalogue shows what a stamp is 'worth'; rather, it shows the price at which Stanley Gibbons will sell a 'fine example' of the stamp. This is perhaps why stamp collectors have complained when some of their prized collectables have achieved just a fraction of the price listed by Stanley Gibbons when it actually came to a sale. The only stamps that appear to generate decent returns regularly for investors are the rare ones – of which fewer than 100 were ever printed, for example. The rule of thumb is that the scarcer the stamp, the more it's worth.

The rarer the stamp, the higher the price tag

The world's most valuable stamp is the 1856 British Guiana Magenta, of which there is only one surviving. This stamp was created by the local postmaster after the boat carrying stamps from the UK was delayed. In 2014, this stamp was auctioned in New York for $9.5 million (£6.4 million), despite being barely legible and in appalling condition. While rare stamps may seem a secure investment, their value can be driven down if many more are suddenly unearthed. There is also the issue of forgery: stamps should have a documented history and certificate of provenance.

Investors who are keen to start amassing a collection of stamps can either use online platforms, such as ukphilately.org.uk or stampworld.com, to source stamps, or invest in dedicated stamp funds, which buy and sell them on your behalf – for a fee, of course. Stanley Gibbons offers this service, but investors must pledge a minimum of £10,000, which will be tied up for between five and ten years. After the set period has elapsed, if the portfolio – typically of between five and ten rare stamps – has increased in value, it can be sold, and Stanley Gibbons takes 20% of the profit.

Is there any point collecting today's rare stamps for future generations to cash in on? Possibly, but so many are printed these days that it is only really worth buying the first-day covers – special envelopes or cards that feature the stamps and are issued on the first day of release. You can buy these at most post offices or order them direct from Royal Mail.

There was a scramble to buy the recent set of Darth Vader stamps, released in December 2015 to herald the release of *Star Wars: The Force Awakens*. Of course, we won't know whether these have appreciated in value for many years yet. Errors could be a better bet, however: stamps that are printed and then subsequently recalled or pulled from sale when mistakes are found. In 1918, a US stamp that has become known as the 'Inverted Jenny' was printed, featuring a stunt plane, which was accidentally printed upside down. Just 700 got into circulation, priced at 24 cents. One of these errors was auctioned off in New York for $825,000 in 2007. By comparison, a corrected version of the stamp changes hands for just $100.

Make sure that stamps make up no more than 10% of your investment portfolio, and be reminded that they are not covered by the Financial Conduct Authority, so you will not get money back if your investment falls in value.

Classic watches

The value of classic watches is rising at a pretty healthy clip, up 5% year on year, according to Blowers, which specializes in buying these retro timepieces as investments.

Between 2005 and 2014, the value of top watches rose considerably faster, 86% over the entire period, based on data from the private bank

Coutts. But its recent Passion Index also revealed that 2014 was a terrible year for the timepiece, with a market contraction of 18%.

Despite this blip, some models from Patek Philippe, Cartier, Omega and Rolex have more than doubled in value over the past decade. Not even the rise of the smartwatch has dented the popularity of some perennial favourites – and there are some nifty ways to ensure that watch investing goes like clockwork.

Seventies and eighties watches seem to have the most potential at the moment. According to Blowers, many timepieces from the sixties and seventies have seen their prices peak and plateau, and are not likely to appreciate much further.

The enduring cool of Steve McQueen

One of the most knowledgeable characters on the watch investment scene is Graham Wilson, one-time music producer – he wrote the nineties hit 'Push The Feeling On' by The Nightcrawlers – turned self-taught timepiece enthusiast and boss of 70s-Watches.com. Any classic watch that has been worn by Steve McQueen is probably a good bet, he reveals – who wouldn't want to own a small piece of the cult cool exuded by the Hollywood star?

The Heuer Monaco that the actor wore on *Le Mans* is one example of a watch that consistently has film buffs and collectors salivating. Other favourites include the Jaeger-LeCoultre Memovox worn by McQueen in *The Thomas Crown Affair* and the Gruen Precision he wore in *The Getaway*. But don't be tempted to buy new versions of these retro watches – TAG Heuer makes lots of modern Steve McQueen reproductions, which look good but will not perform well from an investment perspective.

Wilson says the only brand worn by Steve McQueen that he tends to avoid is the Rolex. McQueen wore his own Rolex Submariner while on set for *Le Mans* and sported a Rolex Speedking in *The Great Escape*, but Rolexes have just become too easy to fake. 'If you're buying a Rolex from the sixties, it's hard to truly know the provenance because parts can be so easily interchanged', says Wilson. 'It's harder to fake parts in an older Omega or Breitling, so you're more likely to find something that is original and will appreciate in value.'

Blowers, in contrast, cites the 30–35% increase in retail prices for new Rolexes over the past six years. 'The price increases have a positive effect on the price of the second-hand watches', claims Mark Blowers, the second generation of the family to run the eponymous business. 'Take the Rolex Submariner, as worn by James Bond. The eighties version looks very similar to the modern watch, and we charged £3,300 for one, while new it was £5,700. If our client wants to sell the classic watch in five years, I would be confident we would allow £3,500 for a part-exchange, even over that short term.'

Undervalued niches in classic watches

Technical watches – timepieces that have been designed for driving or diving, among other pastimes – are good bets, too. The most popular ones on 70s-Watches.com are the Sorna Jacky Ickx drivers watch and the Omega Speedster Tropic. The former was changing hands for around £250 four years ago, and now sells for £650, while the latter has soared in value from £1,400 in 2011 to £2,500 in 2015.

Ladies retro watches have not been as popular as men's traditionally, but this could be about to change, experts claim. While 65% of Blowers' sales are for men's watches, the demand for women's watches – albeit frequently bought by men – is creeping up.

But women tend to hang on to their watches, and be less inclined to swap old models for new, according to Blowers. Fashions change, and women are moving away from the big, flashy, jewel-encrusted watches from the high street towards unique, classic brands.

There are several reasons why watches have become popular with investors. The trend began in 2007, when the financial crisis hit and people became very nervous about having all their wealth tied up in funds or the financial markets. Like jewellery and diamonds, watches are a highly portable commodity – something that is very valuable to a spooked investor. Watches are also not affected by currency fluctuations; you can take them anywhere in the world and sell them.

Watches can be faddy things. When Johnny Depp wore a green Gisa Direct Time on screen in the film *Dark Shadows*, even though it was only really visible for a few seconds, 70s-watches.com was swamped with enquiries. If you're going to become a serious watch investor, be prepared to put in the hours reading up on models and chatting to dealers.

Art

Art dealers are forever claiming that their wares make good investments – is it worth adding a few paintings or sculptures to your portfolio? It depends very much on the kind of art you're looking to collect – and your budget.

It has been claimed that fine art has increased in value by as much as 10% a year over the past four decades, but a recent analysis by the Luxembourg School of Finance of the University of Luxembourg places this figure at closer to 6%.

In 2014, the global art market was worth more than €51 billion worldwide, a 7% increase on the previous year, according to a report by The European Fine Art Foundation. This is an all-time high, beating the last peak in 2007, when the market was worth €48 billion.

The same report showed record demand for art in the UK – good news for domestic art investors. In fact, the UK art market grew 17% in 2014, following years of muted growth. There's still room to grow further, as the UK's current market value of €11.2 billion is still a fair way below its 2008 peak. Yet a separate report, this time by Deloitte, the professional services firm, suggests a softening in demand in 2015, mostly because consumers have been spooked by dodgy economic conditions across Europe, the United States and China.

The art market is completely polarized, however. At the top end, a few works – the Picassos, Pollocks and Gauguins – are changing hands for vast sums, giving the impression of a massive industry when in fact there are a relatively small number of artists, buyers and sellers doing deals. In 2014, the volume of sales grew by 6%, but the number of transactions was still a far cry from the peak of the market in 2007.

The 2014 Art & Finance report, compiled by Deloitte Luxembourg and market research firm ArtTactic, found that 76% of art buyers were picking art and collectables for investment purposes. This compares to just half of buyers in 2012. The most expensive pieces of art are generally viewed as a way to hold wealth, rather than investments to increase in value over time, although this is often a happy coincidence.

The three most important auction houses in the world for art are Christie's, Sotheby's and Bonhams.

Art: the ultimate passion investment?

Investment experts argue among themselves over the merits of putting cash into art; beauty is in the eye of the beholder, after all. Some say that art should be bought for enjoyment alone, and point out that art investments are unregulated, so if the deal goes sour, investors can't go crying to the FSCS.

Selling a work of art on requires a willing buyer, which makes this market rather illiquid. Lastly, you'll probably need to pay for specialist advice on what and when to buy, not to mention the transaction, insurance and storage costs.

Despite the warnings, many investors find art a rewarding part of their overall portfolio. The value of art doesn't rise or fall in tandem with the equity markets, which is a benefit, and it has been shown to be an effective hedge when inflation is rising.

Spotting tomorrow's Picasso

The reason why art may be of interest to the retail investor – and not just the millionaires – is that art sales are now rising steadily at the affordable end of the spectrum, as enthusiasts eschew reproductions in favour of originals by emerging artists.

Sarah Ryan, who founded online art dealer New Blood Art in 2004, trawls the graduate shows and emerging art exhibitions year-round looking for new talent. She has picked several winners over the past decade: you could have bought a large-scale piece by Orlanda Broom for £500 five years ago. One of her lush, colourful landscapes now fetches £15,000. Contemporary artists Iain Andrews and Enzo Marra have also seen the value of their work rise by 1,000% since 2011. To give you an idea of how tough it is to pick winners,

Londonart, an online dealer, points out that there are 1 million artists in the UK – and only around 100 will achieve superstar status at any one time.

Investing in works of art by new talent is an art in itself, Ryan admits, but there three ways that investors can improve their chances of picking a winner. The first thing to do is get to know the artists and their entire body of work. You want to see a stylistic coherence throughout, something that shows the artist has his or her own voice and visual language. You also want to get a handle on how committed the artist is to their creative endeavour. Lots of artists fall at the first hurdle after art college, when money is tight. If they don't continue to make work, they will never become well known and their pieces are far less likely to rise in value. Investors are also advised to look at the quality of the materials used in the painting, sculpture or drawing. There is a whole range of paint qualities, for example, and you want to make sure that the pigment used will maintain its intensity over time. Make sure that good-quality canvas or linen has been used for paintings to be sure that it won't tear or break, devaluing the work.

Beware emotional blackmail – experts have told me that savvy artists can be very persuasive, but don't buy unless you actually love the work.

How to invest in new art

You can either use an emerging art dealer – online players tend to charge lower commissions – or do some scouting yourself. Good starting points are the Affordable Art Fair, Frieze Art Fair, Cameron Contemporary Art's (CCA) exhibition between 25 April and 25 May in Brighton and Hove, and Saatchiart.com. Try attending showcases at the Royal Academy of Art or Central St Martins.

You can be a lone wolf in the art world, picking up pieces that you like, that you feel will be good investments – you may have an eye, who knows. Most people prefer more of a pack mentality. Momentum tends to build around a particular artist very quickly, as a few sales in quick succession create a snowball effect. According to Ryan, as soon as an artist is featured in the press, or a particular image is used for something in the public eye, it always becomes instantly popular, and the seller is swamped with eager buyers. In short, we are lemmings – remember this when devising your art investment strategy, and guard against buying things just because other people are doing so – bubbles can burst.

If you don't want to actually buy and store art, you can try to invest in an art fund. This is easier said than done, as the majority of these funds are offshore and hard to access. This industry has a pretty bad reputation: it's entirely unregulated and highly speculative with precious little transparency – an investing Wild West. At the moment the niche is worth around $1.3 billion, which is a tiny fraction of the overall fund market.

In the UK, there are a couple of investment organizations to consider: The Fine Art Fund Group and Fine Art Wealth Management. The Fine Art Fund Group has $500 million in assets under contract, and requires a minimum investment of $500,000 to $1 million. It claims that its funds have produced an average return of 9% before fees. Art funds charge a management fee of between 1% and 3%, and will take a cut of profits. The Fine Art Fund Group collects its 20% cut of the profit after clients have earned at least 6%. These groups can also help art enthusiasts to buy works as part of a consortium of other investors.

The hot pockets in today's art scene

The term 'art' is incredibly broad and annoyingly vague. Different pockets of the art world boast very different results. According to the private bank Coutts, traditional Chinese works of art have been some of the most profitable pieces of fine art in recent years, almost doubling in value since 2008. Chinese investors and collectors are increasingly looking to buy a piece of their heritage, a phenomenon that has intensified as China's wealth has increased. It's tricky for Westerners to get involved as, typically, they are looking to buy pieces that have been owned privately by Chinese families for hundreds of years. In 2015, demand from the Chinese market cooled – again, the crackdown on bribes and gift-giving has been blamed. This is likely to be a short-term blip: 10 years ago, Sotheby's, the venerable auction house, said that Asia accounted for just 5% of global art sales. Now it represents more than a third.

For those with very deep pockets, Impressionist artists never seem to go out of fashion. For those on tighter budgets, one hot tip is to consider female photographers – this seems to be a popular niche at the moment.

Conclusion

If you need to rebalance your portfolio because it's falling a little short of your targets, or if any of these specialist investments really capture your imagination, it could be worth putting a small proportion of your capital into the options found in this chapter. Many of the investments here are passion investments, and the rules on passion investing are clear: never invest more than 10–20% of your wealth in these assets, and much less if you are on a limited budget.

The benefits of including passion investments in your portfolio is that they tend to provide an inflation hedge, and a tangible asset to offset against your intangible investments, which will make up the majority of your portfolio. Never forget that passion investments are extremely hard to value, especially against traditional equities and income investments, as much of their worth is subjective, and down to what a buyer would be willing to pay. Just because something is hard to value does not mean that the thing necessarily has value.

There are very few data on how many people have lost money on their passion investments: human nature dictates that these investors are reluctant to share this kind of information. But that doesn't mean it doesn't happen. However, if you take a long-term view, choose your investment wisely and aim for something rare, the best in its field, there's no reason why you shouldn't make a healthy return.

High risk and highly specialist

05

It is said that it takes 10,000 hours to become an expert at almost anything. Many of the investments in this section of the book require that kind of dedication – and there really are no shortcuts, unless you happen to know a specialist dealer who both knows the market and doesn't want to make a profit out of you – a truly rare beast.

These investments don't just generate financial rewards – indeed, many investors see the monetary returns as incidental. They can bring real joy to the people who devote themselves to learning about the niche. By becoming a collector of rare musical instruments, for example, they get to play something beautiful every day – although some stock brokers derive similar pleasure from watching share prices rise and fall. These kinds of passion investments also can mean making new friends, expanding horizons – and, of course, showing off. If these are predominantly lifestyle assets, just make sure you can comfortably afford them.

The ultimate test of whether you have chosen the right risk profile to suit your individual tolerance is this: will you sleep easy at night?

Movie memorabilia

Movie merchandise is a sprawling category, comprising original film posters, soft toys, mugs, copies of original screenplays, original props, and much more.

There isn't a huge amount of liquidity in many of these kinds of item – original clothing from a movie, for example, whereas posters could prove an easier find, as many will be printed to advertise new releases.

Prospective investors will not be surprised to hear that perennial classics such as James Bond (Sean Connery-era Bond films are best), Hitchcock and Star Wars tend to generate memorabilia that does well at auction. The most valuable piece of film memorabilia on record is the 1964 Aston Martin driven by Connery in *Goldfinger* and *Thunderball*, which was sold to a private US collector in 2010 for $4,107,560.

In markets like this, soaked in nostalgia, you need only two fans for an auction to have a successful sale. Never underestimate the power of people's desire to own a piece of popular cinema history.

This has been a prominent market for only around half a century. In 1970, Metro Goldwyn Meyer sold off thousands of items, and it is believed that this is the first time collectors began viewing such items as investments.

Hollywood's prizes

Today, Bonhams holds regular film memorabilia sales, while Christie's, Sotheby's and Coys all have ad hoc events. Bonhams recently auctioned off the piano from *Casablanca*, on which Sam played the iconic tune 'As Time Goes By'. It sold for $3.413 million. Other interesting artefacts sold by the auction house include: a Golden Ticket from the 1971 film *Willy Wonka & the Chocolate Factory*, starring Gene Wilder, for £25,000, and the dress Judy Garland wore to play Dorothy in *The Wizard of Oz* back in 1939 for £1.11 million.

As you can tell by these valuations, a lot of movie memorabilia is priced highly, but that does not mean the whole category is out of reach for the casual investor. You may need to buy low and hang on to the item until the market matures; things that cost £100 to buy will still be worth £100 for years, even decades, and then may suddenly appreciate to several thousand pounds.

Fans are still picking up original posters promoting *Harry Potter and the Philosopher's Stone* for less than £200. Compare this to a poster for the 1927 film *Metropolis*, made by Fritz Lang, which sold at auction for almost $700,000 a decade ago.

You need deep pockets to buy James Bond memorabilia from the Connery days, but it may be worth picking up a few bits and pieces associated with Daniel Craig – a new generation may prize this 007's memorabilia highly one day, too.

Film posters: goldmine or waste paper?

Looking at posters generally, originals are always more valuable than reprints. Like newspapers, they were never intended to be kept, so they were usually papered over with new ads, or thrown away, which means that not that many may survive, adding to their value. Tears, trimmed margins and deep creases can affect the value of these products.

Many original posters in decent condition are available for between £1,000 and £1,500, and have the fringe benefit that they actually look great on your wall while being a decent investment. Just remember to keep them out of direct sunlight – you don't want your prized poster to fade.

There is a huge gulf between posters at the top and bottom end of the market. The low end has been flooded with posters over the past 30 years because so many thousands have been printed. According to insiders, this is a good time to buy posters from the fifties and sixties, as these are likely to appreciate over the next five years. If you have only £5,000 or so to spend, a few Bond posters, or classics like *The Godfather*, could be worth more money if stashed away for a while.

Many factors can combine to give each piece their worth – and some of these are down to pure chance. Take the *Spider-Man* film poster, which features the Twin Towers reflected in Spider-Man's eyes. After the 9/11 attack, this became a collectors' item and originals were worth £600 overnight.

Try befriending the popcorn seller at your local cinema, as posters are often thrown away when no longer needed, and this is an opportunity to get one for free.

Cult classics

If you don't manage to pick up an original James Bond, Hitchcock, Godfather, Jaws, or Star Wars poster or piece, look to the films that inspire a whole generation. Take *Withnail and I*. The 1986 film, starring Richard E Grant and Richard Griffiths, is such a cult classic that it has spawned its own collectors' term – Withnalia. Props, posters and memorabilia featured in the film seem consistently to fetch sky-high prices. Three thoroughly nondescript Victorian pine library ladders from the film, which were estimated to be worth £800, were sold for £2,250 in 2011, while Uncle Monty's Cumbrian cottage, which was totally derelict, smashed its £145,000 estimate to sell for £265,000 in 2009. Another tip is 1930s horror films. These iconic images have timeless appeal.

Several things can inflate the value of movie memorabilia: an anniversary – ideally a big one – of the film, the death of one of its stars or a new film from the franchise. It will be interesting to see how old memorabilia from the cult classic *Bill & Ted's Excellent Adventure* (1989) will perform once the latest sequel comes out, for example.

If you're looking to get into the film memorabilia game, have a nose around Moviebits.co.uk, a specialist auction site with a wide range of different kinds of products to get a feel for prices and popular items. Reelposter.com has been selling original film posters for 20 years, and TheCollectorsLot.com has a wide range of signed celebrity photos, if that's your interest. If you want to be really ahead of the curve, try looking at cinema from around the world – Bollywood memorabilia is growing in value and the Chinese market may become very interesting. Online auction sites are also full of memorabilia, but be careful of trusting provenance claims made on eBay – there are many fakes.

Barbies

If you're going to start buying and selling Barbie dolls, the vintage ones seem to be the best bet. Why? Because the cost of a basic modern Barbie has actually decreased when you account for inflation. There have been about 1 billion Barbie dolls sold since 1959, when she was first created.

A good litmus test for assessing demand is always a quick eBay search. I spotted one set of five retro dolls, all made in the early sixties, in mint condition, listed for £7,500 – with almost 200 people watching the item to bid later.

The original Barbie came in both blonde and brunette, but the blonde proved such a hit with little girls that the brunette was quickly consigned to the history books.

Dolled up valuations

The original blonde Barbie is worth an estimated $27,450, according to Forbes, if in mint condition, but the chances of stumbling across one of those at a £1 car boot sale are slim. Nevertheless, it's worth knowing that the first Barbie dolls to be released were the 'Vintage Ponytail Barbie dolls'. These were made between 1959 and 1966 in seven different styles: the original wears a black and white striped swimsuit, and this is the most valuable, even though Mattel has reproduced this Barbie on many occasions since.

You may be able to spot a vintage Bubblecut Barbie, which was sold from 1961 to 1967, because of her resemblance to Jackie Kennedy. The former First Lady first popularized the bubblecut hairstyle, which is now uncannily similar to the sweeping fringe and teased hair sported by East London (male) hipsters.

One vintage Swirl Ponytail Barbie, which was released in 1964, recently sold on eBay for £200, even though she was unboxed, stark naked and damaged by several bite marks on her calves and feet. Modern vintage Barbies date from 1967 to 1972 and are still highly collectable, although less valuable than older versions.

A search for 'vintage Barbie' online should generate a pretty comprehensive list of your investment options. Fashion-doll-guide.com is a good place to start your research.

Here are some things that a canny investor should be aware of. First, the 1960s dolls are far more fragile than their modern equivalents. Always check to make sure that joints function properly, and aren't simply glued in place. Similarly, some unscrupulous sellers may attempt to repaint make-up or mask discolourations, but this drastically reduces the value of the doll. As with any toy, the most valuable vintage Barbies are those still in their original clothing and packaging, with all original accessories still intact.

It's not all about the doll herself; there's a thriving Barbie accessories and clothing market, too. The black and white striped swimsuit referenced earlier is highly collectable.

Barbie's friends are also highly prized by collectors. The vintage Ken was introduced in 1961, her best pal Midge arrived in 1962 and Barbie even got a sister in 1964, with the introduction of Skipper.

Modern classics?

If you are going to take a punt on modern Barbies, holiday-themed dolls seem to be the safest way to go. On Amazon, one mint-condition 2009 Holiday Barbie doll in a shimmering pale pink and golden lamé gown is selling for £110, while a 1993 Winter Princess Barbie Christmas Doll – the first in the series – has an £85 price tag.

If you're going to invest in any of the modern dolls, the quirkier the better. Interesting outfits, and 'themes', tend to prove eye-catching collectables, such as the Barbie 1966 Pan American Airways Stewardess, which recently sold for £80. Professional Barbie collectors keep their stash of dolls in climate-controlled drawers, removing all jewellery (which can cause discolouration) and even keeping the doll separate from the box, wrapped in acid-free tissue paper to make sure that she stays moisture-free.

To learn more about the cult of Barbie, it may be worthwhile attending some of the events dedicated to her fans. If you happen to be heading over to the sunshine state in July 2017, you could hit the National Barbie Doll Collectors Convention in Jacksonville. In the UK, the London International Antique Doll, Teddy Bear and Toy Fair will be held in Olympia in November 2017. Just make sure you don't accidentally end up at Dollcon, also in London. This is the conference for fetishists who want to be a doll, rather than buy a doll.

Military memorabilia

Few investors put their money into medals and other military memorabilia without having some sort of personal interest in their history or provenance. This emotional attachment means that looking at this area of investment breaks my own rules about collectables versus investables, but there have been some extraordinary sales of war memorabilia and medals in recent years, which means that these assets cannot be ignored.

According to various online collectors' marketplaces, the value of medals and other military memorabilia has risen fivefold over the past 20 years. At the end of the nineties, a Victoria Cross could be bought for between £50,000 and £80,000, but in 2010, one sold for £327,000. Prices rise far higher, too; in 2009, Lord Ashcroft, a leading collector of these medals, paid £1.5 million for the 'ultimate' gallantry medal – the only double Victoria Cross from the Great War. Interestingly, Lord Ashcroft's interest in Victoria Crosses seems to have been one of the driving forces behind rising prices. Bonhams, the London auction house that holds specialist auctions in military items, otherwise known as militaria, is more conservative about the market's growth, saying only that over the past 30 years, there have been gradual increases in values.

How to spot valuable militaria

This is a sprawling investment area, encompassing vintage uniforms, antique weapons, medals, and even accessories such as old water bottles and battlefield first-aid kits. As a rule, the value of military memorabilia tends to lie chiefly in its condition, the quality of the workmanship and its historical significance, or stories attached to the item.

There is no shortcut to success with militaria. Experts advise steeping yourself thoroughly in the market, attending as many antique fairs, military museum exhibits and auctions as possible. No bidding in the early days; this is just a learning exercise. Also take a look at the quarterly catalogues from the likes of the auctioneers Spink, DNW and Bosley's. Spink even has a smartphone app.

Most specialist auctions take place in London, which is the centre of militaria trading. There are between eight and ten of these specialist events held each year in the capital.

There are few concrete trends in the militaria market, but experts admit that key events can help drive up the value of militaria. It is believed, for example, that the bicentenary of the Battle of Waterloo, which fell in June 2015, helped spur sales of associated memorabilia. There were several auctions arranged to coincide with the anniversary, and one at Bonhams saw several lots beat their estimates by some margin.

A George IV 18-carat gold Irish Freedom Box made by Edward Murray of Dublin in 1827, which was owned by Lord Uxbridge, the first Marquess of Anglesey (the level of detail here explains why prospective investors must do their homework), sold for £100,900 on an estimate of just £50,000 to £70,000. Of course, the chap who bought this may not be a collector of military items, but of gold boxes.

Still, the 'very fine and rare presentation sabre that was given to Thomas Harris by Edward Solly in commemoration of their fellowship at the memorable battle of Leipzig' – from the same auction – sold for almost £44,000, with a lower estimate of £35,000.

Medals are an interesting subset of militaria, and a collectors' favourite. Rarer medals are, understandably, worth the most. Infantry medals are scarce, which means they are more valuable than artillery medals. There are very few cavalry medals, too, and these are particularly sought after if in good condition; the battering they received when worn on horseback means that they tend to be more bashed up than infantry medals. Beware of forgeries in this era of laser printing.

Vintage weapons

There has also been much interest in flintlock and percussion weapons in recent years. I wonder if this has anything to do with the fact that 'English Percussion Flintlock Pistols' are one of the hidden treasures in the 2014 videogame, *Assassin's Creed Rogue*. Laugh if you want, but certain shoot 'em ups have helped youngsters today learn more about guns than they ever would have otherwise, creating a new generation of collectors.

Flintlock weapons were introduced in the 17th century, and are fired by a spark from a flint. The percussion cap was invented in the 19th century, and was an improvement on the flintlock as it allowed the pistols of old to fire reliably in any weather. I found a pair of original mid-17th-century flintlock muskets on sale for $10,000 on Collectorsfirearms.com. Even the reproduction muskets make a pretty penny, selling for around £400 online.

Roughly speaking, the sweet spot for these guns is between 1880 and 1950. The value of vintage guns worth £5,000 or less has remained pretty flat over the past few years, according to Sotheby's, but those that are worth more than £10,000 have become increasingly popular as investments, causing their prices to rise.

It's important to be aware of the rules governing owning firearms in the UK. Anyone who owns a 'cartridge weapon' – something firing a bullet or shot – will need to have a Firearms Certificate unless the weapon is so old that the ammunition is no longer available – you can check this out on the Home Office list of obsolete calibres. You are fine to own any kind of muzzle loader – these guns have some form of projectile loaded at the front – as long as it was manufactured before the Second World War. Look out for a reference to 'Section 58(2)' (this refers to the Firearms Act of 1968) in dealers' lists and auction house catalogues to be on the safe side.

Violins

Violins have proven to be one of the safest investments out there – if you can afford one. The most valuable models were made before 1800, which means there's a finite number, helping to make this a very stable asset class. The fact that these instruments are in demand because musicians actually want to play them helps to add to their allure.

Experts tell me that an Italian violin of good pedigree and sound, which is at least a hundred years old, is always a good investment. As time marches on, later models have also become more attractive: violins from around 1850 cost around $500,000, which, though expensive, is a fraction of the price of older models – $5 million for a classic Stradivarius. The most expensive violin ever sold was the Vieuxtemps, made by the 18th-century Italian luthier Giuseppe Guarneri del Gesù, which fetched $16 million at auction.

The price of classic violins – those worth $100,000 or more – grows at around 10% per year, according to an analysis of sales data from 1970 by Florian Leonhard Fine Violins. If you can afford a Stradivarius, these appreciate by more than 15% a year. Like art or other vintage collectables, there isn't a huge amount of liquidity in the market – not that many top violins will come to auction. Banks and other institutions have begun buying up violins because they have proved such stable investments, which means there's lots of competition for top instruments. When they do come to auction, beware of the fees charged by the auction houses. You'll also have to insure the thing, which can be 0.5–2% of the value of the instrument.

Figure 5.1 Index comparison for all asset classes, 1980–2012

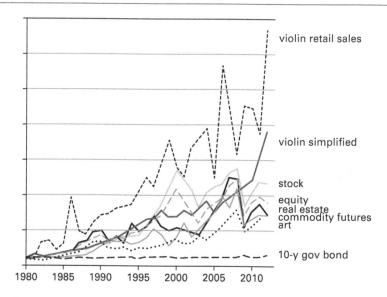

SOURCE: *The Economist*

It is advisable to hold a violin for two to five years in order to realize a return on investment, but these instruments can also just be used to store wealth in the long term.

Investing in new violins

For those with smaller budgets, more modern violins aren't a bad investment. A 1900 Stefano Scarampella violin, which was bought for $12,000 in the eighties, was sold for $150,000 some 20 years later. The things to look out for are: who made it; the quality; who owned it in the past;

current fashions; and actual sound. Cheaper violins will appreciate by only around 3% each year, unless you're lucky enough to find a particularly popular maker, or one that has a wonderful story around it.

Always buy the cleanest, healthiest instrument that your budget allows – bashed-up models, even from fashionable makers, are slower to appreciate in value. Don't try to find these violins on eBay; this is a complex area, so you want to deal only with reputable dealers. There are thousands of fakes on the market, and as modern manufacturing techniques become more sophisticated, it is harder and harder to tell the originals from the copies. Some of the fakes are even crafted from vintage wood, which means they even befuddle attempts to use dendrochronology to date the instrument.

If you can't afford a violin on your own, or want to invest a smaller sum but still shoot for a classic violin, you could form a syndicate. Florian Leonhard Fine Violins runs several syndicates, with investors putting in a minimum of £5,000.

Instruments were meant to be played

If your violin is played by an artist who subsequently becomes famous, the value could soar. There's also the thrill of being able to hear your precious violin being played, which is more rewarding than keeping it under glass. On a more practical note, if you lend a violin to an orchestra or university, they will typically cover the cost of the insurance, which can reduce your bills. It is also said that these instruments benefit from being played, as the vibrations from bowing and strumming bring the violin to life.

The violin market has been boosted by a surge in Asian investors. It is estimated that 30 million Chinese people are learning the violin at any one time, and they may then blossom into violin connoisseurs and investors.

Don't forget that bows are also an interesting investment, with some older bows – sans hair just wood – fetching $400,000 or more. There isn't as much data about the performance of bow prices, but anecdotally, some top bows that sold for $2,000 a few years ago are now worth about $8,000.

Alongside violins, cellos and violas are also interesting investments – albeit the market for these is dwarfed by the demand for violins.

There is also far less liquidity in violas, for example. There are only 10 known Stradivarius violas in existence – how's that for limited liquidity? This compares to about 600 Stradivarius violins.

Guitars

Vintage guitars are a sexy investment but, like violins, you'll need deep pockets to get into this market. The top instruments, made by the likes of Gibson in the fifties and sixties, are worth millions and are growing in value by around 15% each year.

Among the most valuable vintage guitars, based on sales data from the past few years, are: the 1958–59 Explorer and 1958–60 Les Paul Standard, both made by Gibson; the 1936–42 Martin D-45; and D'Aquisto archtops. Vintage Rickenbackers, Gretsch and Guild guitars are also appreciating in value.

What do we mean by vintage? This generally means that the guitars were made from materials or using techniques that were later changed, making them more precious. Leo Fender, inventor of the eponymous – and legendary – electric guitar, sold his business in 1965, which means that guitars made before this time are highly prized.

Provenance has become one of the most crucial ways of determining the value of a vintage guitar – has one of the all-time greats played it? Eric Clapton's old axes are by far the most valuable, breaking previous records each time they come to auction, with one – 'Blackie', which is built from three vintage Stratocasters – selling for almost $1 million. It is worth noting that Blackie was something of an anomaly – typically, 'hacked' guitars will see their value plunge.

The most valuable guitar of all time, selling for $2.7 million in 2005, is a Fender Stratocaster that was sold off to raise money for the tsunami relief effort. It was signed by 20 top artists, including members of The Who, The Beatles, The Rolling Stones and – you guessed it – Eric Clapton.

The Clapton effect

It could be his reputation as one of the best guitarists of all time, but could just be a result of his sway over the market. Clapton is a prolific collector of top vintage guitars and once sold off 100 at once to raise money for his Crossroads Centre charity, which helps people affected by drug and alcohol abuse.

Guitars owned by members of The Beatles, Bob Marley, Bob Dylan, The Rolling Stones or Jimi Hendrix are also highly collectable. Following his death in 2016, it's likely that David Bowie's instruments will soar in value, especially if the auctions take place at the same time as big exhibitions or tribute shows.

By far the biggest market for these guitars is the United States, so it is typically artists who were big across the pond that attract the attention of collectors. Baby boomers – those born between 1946 and 1964 – now control most of the world's wealth, so it's worth considering which 'rock gods' were popular during their partying days.

According to the 42-Guitar Index (Figure 5.2), which is based on the sales of vintage Fender, Gibson and Martin models, prices peaked in 2008, as Wall Street financiers ploughed their wealth into physical assets before the credit crunch hit. After that, the numbers plunged by 30%, languishing at an average of $700,000 in 2013.

Over the past three years, however, there has been a slow but steady uptick and prices are now approaching $800,000. They are forecast to grow by an average of 1% each year for the next three years.

Figure 5.2 The 42-Guitar Index, 1991–2016

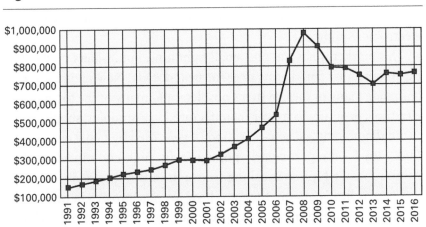

While top Gibsons go for a song at auction, the prices of mid-range models can be volatile, and the same applies to Fenders. Acoustic Martins tend to hold their value more than rival brands, at least based on historic data. There have been bubbles in this market before, where speculators buy up vintage guitars just to 'flip' them – sell them on quickly – creating an artificial buzz around the market and driving up prices.

How to pick the right guitar

If you do decide to get into this market, only work with reputable dealers as there are a lot of fakes out there. Buy the best Fender, Gibson or Martin vintage guitar that you can afford, and make sure that it is not only in excellent original condition but includes the original guitar case. If the instrument is considered to be an investment, allow 10 years for the instrument to appreciate – and be sure to play the instrument every so often. Make sure your instruments are stored properly – guitars can warp if exposed to humidity, for example – and get them insured to protect your investment.

Techno gear

Many of the rock stars of yesteryear were 'shredders', creating massive demand for vintage guitars. But many of the hit musicians of the modern era are using drum machines, samplers, sequencers and synthesizers to create top tracks. This has given rise to a new market for electronic equipment.

This market is nascent and small right now, but insiders predict that the opportunity could grow over the next decade. New digital software has made many of these systems obsolete, and many of the top pieces of electronic gear are no longer manufactured, constraining supply.

Analogue synthesizers – the kind of gear used by Led Zeppelin and Pink Floyd – are particularly popular, with high-end models such as Minimoogs or Jupiter-8s selling for thousands of pounds.

There is little data out there to show average growth in prices – the market really is that new – but anecdotally, a Yamaha CS-80, a vintage polysynth, now changes hands for $15,000 and it cost $6,900 new in 1976. Those in possession of vintage equipment like this tend to make private sales, which makes the details hard to find. Some of the most valuable pieces are in seriously short supply: the most valuable drum machine out there is the EKO ComputeRhythm, of which only 20 were ever sold. *Attack Magazine*, which focuses on dance music and culture, claimed in its October 2013 issues that prices of analogue equipment have been rising since the 1990s, driven by demand from producers seeking an authentic and retro sound. The magazine published an annual list of the most desirable electronic gear, with average asking prices, so you can compare how like models have performed over the years.

Not all synthesizers are born equal

The PPG WAVE, the synthesizer used by David Bowie and Trevor Horn, cost $7,000 in 1981, and, according to various forums, they now cost between $2,000 and $2,500. That said, musicians are asking for vintage synthesizers with increasing frequency and these are harder and harder to find on auction sites such as eBay, so the price could soon soar. Make sure that when considering an analogue synth, you look at the price – and reputation – of its digital grandchild. If the new model has generated great reviews and is cheaper than the analogue version, you may struggle to shift your model.

If the equipment has been used by a famous artist or band, its value could double. Brian Eno's EMS Synthi AKS sold for £17,000 in 2013, more than twice the typical price. It could be worth keeping an eye on what the up-and-coming stars of today are using in the studio; picking up their old equipment could reap rewards down the line.

It's important to know that advancements in technology have actually driven down the prices of many retro electronic products – some samplers from the seventies and eighties have actually lost value, because there is now digital software that makes it much easier to record and loop music. But does this mean that we should buy up cheap samplers now because they will become valuable in the future, once the 'vintage is better than now' craze hits that particular niche? Only time will tell. If we think of electronic gear as following in the wake of other analogue markets, such as vintage cameras, there is likely to be a dip for many years, and then a spike in value.

This is not an easy market to get into. So much depends on getting a good price for your synth or drum machine up front, which means you need connections – and you probably have to be in the right place at the right time. Electronic gear also needs a lot of tender loving care. It is extremely hard to fix when it breaks down, and a broken synth is almost worthless. There is also a lot of ill-will out there for investors who buy up top-end equipment as a cash cow, rather than because they want to make music. This is an age-old ethical dilemma: are you actually preventing a talented musician from creating something incredible with your synth, which is sitting in a sealed box in your basement? The decision is yours.

Comic books

In February 2016, a near-mint 1969 edition of *Amazing Fantasy*, the first comic that Spider-Man ever appeared in, was sold for $454,000. It cost just 12 cents when it was first sold. Back in 2011, another one of those comics sold to a private investor for $1.1 million.

This is nothing compared to *Action Comics* #1, the 1938 comic that introduces Superman and Lois, and is now worth $3 million. It's enough to send investors scrabbling through attics, basements and garages looking for old stashes.

Unfortunately, the majority of comics from the past few decades are practically worthless. This was the warning issued by Kevin Maroney, a US collector who has invested hundreds of thousands of dollars in almost 30,000 different issues over the years – and is now struggling to offload his collection. 'Comics are not a good investment', he told Bloomberg, the news agency. 'Most comic books are worth literally nothing.'

The world's most valuable comics

The few that are worth something are incredible investments. According to GoCompare.com, a select few have outperformed the share prices of the top 500 US companies since 2008. The research found that the top performer was DC's *The Batman Adventures* #12, first published in 1993. Originally sold for $1.25, it's now worth $800, making a 26,567% return. Or look at Marvel's *New Mutants*, which was worth $1 when it was published and now sells for $250. Experts advise that when buying older comic books, look out for first editions where heroes, villains or cult characters are being introduced for the first time. Speculative investors should lean towards comic books that are at least 10 years old and whose characters have seen enduring popularity. Avoid damaged comics, as tears and missing pages can decimate value – there are exceptions, of course, for the super, super rare, which are always valuable, even with tattered edges.

What gives comic books their value and how can today's investors pick the valuable comics of tomorrow? One interesting theme is that comics featured in big blockbusters tend to see a sudden surge in popularity and therefore price. Case in point: The movie *Deadpool*, which was released in 2016, drove up the price of *New Mutants*. It may be worth keeping an eye on upcoming new releases to see which characters are coming to the big screen. The film *Suicide Squad*, which opened in August 2016, is tipped to drive up the price of comics featuring Harley Quinn, Joker's girlfriend in the Batman universe, who is the film's heroine. Collectors say that *The Batman Adventures* #12, published in 1993, is now selling for more than $1,000 because it's the first time we meet Dr Harleen F Quinzel, AKA Harley Quinn. This is an unexpected development – who could have known that this relatively unknown character would get picked out by Hollywood?

Could these be the comic book hits of tomorrow?

Following that logic, comic book collectors will be interested to note that Marvel's Doctor Strange is currently being turned into a film featuring Benedict Cumberbatch in the lead role. Also, the film of Black Panther, another Marvel creation – drawn by the legendary Stan Lee – is tabled to be hitting screens in 2018. Readers first encountered him in *Fantastic Four* #52, published in July 1966. The point here is not that you should dash out and bulk-buy these comics, but to show the workings-out that collectors have to do in order to buy smart.

When it comes to picking winners out of today's comic crop, you want to try to imagine what people will want to read 10 years down the line – and which comics could be turned into big Hollywood franchises. Maroney's statement stands – the vast majority of the comics printed today probably won't be worth much down the road, but there are some authors and illustrators whose works are highly prized, and frequently sell out within days of being published. Brian K Vaughan is certainly one modern writer to watch. He's been called 'the greatest comic book visionary of the last five years' and has worked on big-ticket films and TV shows from *Ex Machina* to *Buffy The Vampire Slayer* and *LOST*. His latest series *Paper Girls*, which costs $9.99, is already fiendishly hard to get hold of, and my mate Gwynne, a comic book collector, has tipped this one for a good investment. He has form in this area. He bought a first edition of *Saga* #1, written by Vaughan and illustrated by Fiona Staples, for a couple of pounds in 2012. It's now selling for £89.99 on eBay, with some copies carrying a £110 price tag. Oh, and there are also rumours that Marvel, which is now owned by Disney, may eventually make a film based on *Runaways*, a superhero comic book series also written by Vaughan.

Scarcity is one of the main drivers of value

Comic book collectors joke that if their mothers hadn't forced them to throw away so many comics growing up, there would be no market today – we'd be awash in the things. Hot tip when buying comics today: look out for series with a limited run.

Comic books, new and old, are available to buy through many different channels, although eBay seems especially popular. The Florida-based Certifiable Guaranty Company (CGC), set up by husband-and-wife team Scott and Molly Davis in 2000, is also proving an increasingly important cog in the wheel of comic investing. They have made a name for themselves in the business of grading – assigning value to comics. Collectors send their prized books to CGC to be sealed inside an inert plastic case and permanently included in their database with a unique code that can be used to track the comic through its future owners – and is used to prove authenticity. It's worth noting that this grading has been known to drive up the price of comics – compared to ungraded options – but buyers often pay the premium because CGC will then track a book's value over time, creating a sort of unofficial stock exchange for comic books.

Conclusion

Benjamin Graham, the author of *The Intelligent Investor*, one of the most respected books about investing ever written, gives his definition of an 'enterprising' investor not as someone who accepts a high level of risk, but as someone who is willing to put the work in. If this is the case, those pursuing the investments outlined in this chapter are truly the most enterprising of enterprising investors. These are high-risk, mostly illiquid and tricky investment options that require multiple hours of research and a lot of luck to boot. But then Graham also said that an investor should always look for a 'significant margin of safety relative to prices', so he would almost certainly have been horrified by the idea of anyone attempting to profit from comic books or old pistols. It bears repeating that those interested in making any of the investments at this end of the book should limit their spend to a very small percentage of their available capital. If I had £100,000 to play with, or less, I probably wouldn't touch them at all, unless they were going to be part investment, part hobby.

High risk with 06
high returns

The old saying goes, 'You have to speculate to accumulate', and we're at the speculation end of the book now. Speculation is defined as an endeavour that carries a significant risk of losing most or all of your initial investment, in expectation of a substantial gain. Some speculation is educated speculation, based on careful research and an understanding of the market. This is a calculated risk. There are other kinds of speculation that are simply gambling, and those are referenced in this chapter, too.

There is money to be made from speculating, but the risks are manifold. Some of these investment options are very specialist, which means that you have to really know your stuff to make money, others are very nascent and untested – even though early signs are encouraging, it would be foolish to assume that they are safe.

The investment options in this chapter should make up only a very small part of your overall portfolio, and should consist only of money you can lose without any serious repercussions.

Mini-bonds

Like common-or-garden retail bonds, mini-bonds are also a way for private companies to raise money from fans and customers. Like other kinds of crowdfunding, companies state a target amount that they want to hit, and set out their stall for what the money will be used for.

Some companies will then pay their investors regular cash dividends, like other, more run-of-the-mill bonds, while others pay in kind. Confectionery makers may pay their dividend in toffee, for example, before returning the principal in full at the end of the term – typically three to five years down the line.

It's a pretty sweet deal for small companies, which are now able to raise capital without giving away equity in return. In this way, small investors can replace the old bank loan.

Mini-bonds also help ensure that fans always choose the product or service offered by the issuer over a rival's. Mini-bondholders are incentivized to care about the success of the company they back. It's quite a clever ruse, and one that is proving more and more popular.

Not as cute as they sound

Mini-bonds fall pretty high on the risk scale, because they are subject to much looser regulation than corporate or retail bonds. They are also not tradable on the stock market, so you're stuck with them until they mature, or go pop.

Even mini-bonds that are backed by assets may not return your money if the company folds. This is because bondholders may find themselves quite far down the pecking order – other debts may be settled first, leaving investors high and dry. Some issuers do make an effort to safeguard their backers' money, by creating 'secured' bonds, which means that investors have a claim on particular assets in the event of a default.

There have been a couple of instances where companies have issued mini-bonds and been unable to pay back either the interest or the original sum, which has spooked the market. If an issuer does go bust, there is no protection from the government scheme that protects bank customers, the FSCS.

However, there are also many examples of successful bond schemes. The 'shaving bond', created by King of Shaves, the razor and toiletries company, the 'chocolate bond' from Hotel Chocolat and the 'beer bond' from brewery Innis & Gunn, to name a few, have all successfully paid their investors back, or are in the process of doing so. These bonds have given backers up to 7.33% interest, reflecting the risk profile of the investments. Mini-bonds can offer deals with 8% interest or more.

Mini-bonds can be issued outside the UK, too. Madonne Caseificio dell'Emilia, an Italian cheese maker, recently raised €6 million through a 'parmesan bond', which was backed by wheels of the hard cheese.

Mini-bonds hit the mainstream

Mini-bonds hit the mainstream after crowdfunding platform Crowdcube began offering them as part of their product mix. Between June 2014 and November 2015, eight companies raised £10.9 million from more than 3,250 individual investments in bonds on Crowdcube. During that time, five companies paid out £400,000 in interest payments, at a yield of between 6% and 11%. Crowdcube has done quite a lot for mini-bonds' reputation, striking a deal with debt rating firm Moody's Analytics to determine the 'probability of default' of each mini-bond on its platform, and scoring the issuer on its likelihood of default.

Many investment experts are genuinely worried about the rise of mini-bonds, and warn that we will only truly understand how risky they are a few years down the line, after these companies have already burnt through their mini-bond funds. The companies raising money through this mechanism are obliged to warn prospective backers that mini-bonds are only for highly sophisticated investors, yet this remains a self-certification process.

Pioneers in the alternative market believe that mini-bonds have a bright future, and claim that it will become a great way for investors to profit from the success of growing companies. Whichever side of the fence you sit on, make sure that mini-bonds make up only a very small percentage of your portfolio. Only commit your capital to a mini-bond if you are sure that you can't get the same – or even a better – deal with a traditional stock market fund.

Peer-to-peer lending

Handing your precious savings over to strangers and trusting them to pay the full amount back with interest may seem a fool's errand, but the model has exploded in recent years. Early indications show that peer-to-peer (P2P) is highly lucrative, at least for now.

With interest rates exceeding 5%, depending on the platform, P2P outperforms the cash savings products offered by the major high street banks. Some of the riskier platforms offer returns as high as 12% – but, of course, the chances of losing your money are much higher.

In the 10 years since the alternative finance industry first began issuing these P2P loans in the UK, £2.6 billion has been lent out by 100,000 Britons. These early adopters have made around £6,000 each. But the sector is growing incredibly fast; in 2015, the Liberum AltFi Volume Index, which tracks the performance of the whole alternative finance industry, found that £2.81 billion of financing was ploughed into the UK market by armchair investors, a 75.7% uplift on 2014. Of this £2.81 billion, £2.68 billion was debt financing – P2P loans. The rest was invested through equity investments – people backing companies in return for shares.

Platforms claim that these returns are possible because they use technology to do the grunt work in transactions, taking down the cost of each deal, and use credit checks and risk-rating tools to cherry-pick the least dodgy borrowers. There is no bank or other middleman involved, taking a cut, and each investment is often split into tiny sums and lent to multiple borrowers to reduce risk. McKinsey, the consultancy, has said that P2P platforms can offer loans at 400–500 basis points less than a bank can afford to do.

A fair weather investment?

It's fair to say that much of P2P's success has come about because of the favourable economic environment. Broadly speaking, the UK is doing pretty well, and the low-interest-rate environment is still buoying up the economy.

Critics of P2P ask what will happen if interest rates are hiked suddenly, or if the economy goes pop. After all, think about who is borrowing this money and why – usually it's people who can't secure traditional finance, for a variety of reasons. A lot of P2P lending is unsecured, so you could lose some of your investment if a crisis hit. Most of the platforms won't just let you extract your money on a whim – it's locked in for a fixed period, so you won't be able to cash in your chips quickly at the first sniff of a rates rise.

The four biggest P2P lenders are Zopa, RateSetter, Funding Circle and Landbay, which all allow you to start lending in minutes online.

So far, the borrowers' 'default' rate, the proportion of loans that were not repaid, is less than 1% for these major players, but, again, this is while the economy is in rude health.

The bigger P2P lenders also hold capital reserves – just like banks do – which are meant to cover loans that go bad. At Zopa, this is 2% of the total loan book. By April 2017, all of these firms will have to hold at least £50,000 worth of capital – or more for the larger businesses – to act as a buffer.

Zopa and RateSetter are fairly similar, except that RateSetter allows you to reinvest interest as you go, which compounds the return. It also allows you a little wiggle room on the interest rate – on a loan priced at 5%, you can opt to offer 4.9% or 4.8% if you want the money to be taken up a little faster for speedier deals.

Funding Circle lends exclusively to businesses, so it is arguably the most risky. Investors can either choose the firms they want to back – the information about what the loan is for and how well the business is doing is easily accessible – or use Funding Circle's automatic engine, which spreads your investment across a diverse group of borrowers.

Asset-backed investments

There are some specialist P2P lenders who operate only in secured loans. Ablrate is one of these, helping borrowers to buy aircraft or shipping containers, for example. It plays in the funding space ignored by the banks because it's just too small and fiddly (if you can call a £5 million loan fiddly), as opposed to operating on the fringes as many other platforms do.

Similarly, Landbay lends only to people seeking a mortgage, which means they are borrowing against actual physical property – one of the safest asset classes there is – which probably explains why it was the fastest-growing platform in 2015, posting growth of almost 1,000%, albeit from a low base.

There are a couple of ways of investing in Landbay – the three-year-fixed deal, which offers a compound interest rate of 4.47%, or the tracker, which promises investors returns that are at least 3% greater than the Libor rate – the rate at which banks lend each other money – so around 3.65%.

Landbay lent out around £22 million over the 18-month period following its launch in April 2014, with an average loan topping £170,187. There have been no defaults and none of the platform's borrowers are in arrears – although it is early days.

The risks are manifold

As with any exciting new industry, there have been some cowboys coming to market to take advantage of unwary investors. One Chinese outfit, Ezubo, was closed down by the authorities in late 2015, leaving 900,000 investors out of pocket. It is much easier to spot dodgy outfits in the UK, however, as these companies are now regulated by the Financial Conduct Authority.

The whole industry was thrown a bone by the government in 2016 when it was announced that savers could lend their savings via P2P through the newly minted Innovative Finance Isa. This is halfway between a cash Isa and a stocks and shares Isa. You can make returns of up to 6% but you could also lose it all, and your savings aren't covered in this product, the way they are in a cash Isa.

Never invest more than you are prepared to lose in P2P. The older you get, the smaller this investment should be. Make sure you understand exactly where your money is going and how long it will be tied up. If ever there was a time to read the small print, this is it: some lenders offer 'easy access' options, which sound great: 'Give us 28 days' notice and we'll give you back your money!' but a closer look at the rules reveals umpteen caveats that let these platforms wiggle out of that promise.

From April 2016, investors were allowed to include some of the returns from P2P investing in their tax-free Isa. Otherwise the interest you earn is subject to Income Tax, like any earnings.

Junk bonds

You know the basics about corporate bonds, so now we can start looking at their riskier cousins – junk bonds. Junk bonds are issued by companies that have a higher risk of defaulting on their repayments. This may sound scary, but investors can find these investments tempting because they pay a much higher yield to bondholders. In recent years, the yield on junk bonds has been 4–6% higher than US government bonds (arguably the safest bonds you can buy).

These returns are so high because the borrowers have no other option. Their credit ratings are poor, so they can't secure finance using cheaper means. Think of the junk bond as the payday loan, given to borrowers who are down on their luck and forced to accept a high rate of interest. If the junk bond goes bad, the investor gets nothing.

Celestial beings

Junk bonds can be split into two categories. They are either 'fallen angels', so called because they were once investment grade but have been downgraded to junk-bond status because of a company's credit issues, or they are 'rising stars', issued by a company that is on its way up – they are still junk bonds but could be investment grade soon.

Junk bonds can be traded on the London Stock Exchange, just like other corporate or retail bonds, but retail investors rarely touch these bonds because they are hard to access and incredibly risky. The only way to play in this market is through mutual funds, for example. In the main, it's just institutional investors looking to make big returns betting a small percentage on very large piles of junk.

A brief history of junk

Junk bonds first rose to prominence in the late seventies and early eighties. This is when early-stage companies with no access to credit cottoned on to the fact that they could issue junk bonds as a way of securing growth capital.

During the 1980s, an ambitious trader from the investment bank Drexel Burnham Lambert also realized that high-risk, high-return debt instruments were a potential goldmine. His name was Michael Milken, although he was later known simply as 'The Junk Bond King'. He was responsible, almost single-handedly, for giving junk bonds a bad name. He created the junk-bond craze, convincing investors to pile in, and peddled them as a means for companies to fund hostile takeovers, which was frowned upon by the investment world.

These bond issuers didn't have any cash to fund these deals, but the junk bonds gave them the leverage they needed. A decade later, many of these companies were defaulting on their bonds, and scores of investors were burnt. Milken went to prison for securities fraud – although he remains a billionaire to this day.

Distressed securities as a whole

Junk bonds belong to a wider dysfunctional family of 'distressed securities'. This is a catch-all term for all the financial instruments derived from distressed firms, be they bonds, equities, trade receivables or whatever.

Again, as with junk bonds, it would be really unlikely that an investor would want to invest directly in distressed debt, first because it comes in very high denominations, so you'd need something like £250,000 just to enter the market. It's also incredibly difficult to assess the creditworthiness of the company whose instruments you're buying. Not only must you assess the likelihood of being paid back, but you would also need to familiarize yourself with the legal structure around bankruptcy – just in case things don't work out and you need to try to find a way to get your money back. Again, those who want to gamble on distressed securities can do it through a mutual fund, where the risks are diversified.

Cryptocurrencies

A cryptocurrency is a digital currency that uses cryptography – complex codes, the kind used by spies in James Bond movies – to prevent them being counterfeited or stolen. This is money, but a new kind of money, which is not regulated by any single governing body.

The original and most famous cryptocurrency is bitcoin. This was formally introduced in 2009 – you may have heard its name linked with buying drugs or arms on the internet, but the currency has come a long way from its unsavoury past.

Bitcoin was created by 'Satoshi Nakamoto', a pseudonym used by a person or team (we're still not quite sure which) as a peer-to-peer currency that relies on users to keep it working. While bitcoin payments are anonymous, all transactions are recorded in a kind of digital diary, known as the block chain.

Bitcoin, the granddaddy of cryptocurrency, now has many descendants. There are now over 1,500 different currencies, usually using a moniker ending in 'coin', but only a few of them have a market valuation of anything significant. This section will take you through the main currencies vying for investors' money, and explain the risks and rewards for getting involved.

Bitcoin

Bitcoin remains the leading digital currency. Transactions in bitcoins are made by sending an encrypted message signed and locked using a key which is private to the user. This transaction can be verified by others in the network by using a public key. You can see the amount transferred, just not who sent it and where it went. People have embraced the currency as it provides a way to transfer money securely, cheaply and instantly to anyone in the world.

Over the past seven years, the value of a single bitcoin has risen from zero to around £500 at the time of writing. There have been peaks and troughs along the way – the cryptocurrency peaked at around £700 back in 2013 and fell to a low of £150 in 2015.

Should prospective investors be worried about this volatility? One man's threat is another's opportunity. Owing to its volatility and liquidity, bitcoin has become a favourite among speculators, with high-frequency traders and hedge funds piling in.

It doesn't look as if bitcoin is going to stabilize anytime soon either; Andreas M Antonopoulos, a technologist and one of the most respected voices in the bitcoin industry, has said: 'Bitcoin will crash at least twice more before it can mature as a global currency.'

Not a short-term play

Those who are looking to park some money in the currency will need to be patient. It could take years to ride out the month-on-month price fluctuations.

The long-term value of the currency is ensured – its proponents claim – by a quirk of design. There is a cap on the supply of bitcoins.

Once 21 million bitcoins have been mined, the system will stop creating the coins. It is estimated that we will reach this limit in 2140. Market rules dictate that the finite number of coins should drive up their value over the long term. The rate at which they are being mined is also slowing. They are incredibly time-consuming and require enormous computing power to produce, even now. The number of new coins created by the system is set to halve every four years.

There are a few different ways that investors can engage with bitcoins, but insiders tell me that buying bitcoin mining equipment or contracts with third-party companies who rent out mining power are currently not worthwhile and will most likely not show a return on investment until prices push $600. Many people tried to get involved with the bitcoin rush in 2014, and ordered machines known as 'miners' to earn themselves bitcoins. The process of bitcoin mining is a decentralized computational process where miners use their computing power to calculate cryptographic hash functions in order to verify and record payments into a public ledger. In layman's terms, your computer solves complex problems in return for bitcoins. The only problem is, the more miners there are out there, the scarcer the mining work is, and therefore the more difficult it becomes to make money from these rather expensive machines. It is sometimes more lucrative to mine a lesser known cryptocurrency and then convert it into bitcoins than to try to go direct for the original currency.

Bitcoin as a hedge

Some see bitcoins not just as an investment, but as an opportunity to minimize financial risk caused by fluctuating exchange rates. For example, it has been suggested that adding bitcoins to the reserve portfolio of major banks would help offset exchange rate depreciations against major currencies such as the pound and the euro, while providing significant returns because of its appreciation against the dollar.

Bitcoin has begun to shrug off its nefarious connotations; the New York Stock Exchange has launched a Bitcoin index, NYXBT. The Winklevoss twins, the pair who allegedly conceived of Facebook alongside Mark Zuckerberg, have now launched Gemini, a fully licensed and regulated bitcoin exchange, and are currently pushing the

Securities and Exchange Commission to allow them to create a bit-coin ETF. This has been kicked into the long grass, but meanwhile US outfit Ark Invest, which focuses on building ETFs around disruptive innovation, has created its own wrapper, which pulls in bitcoin.

How to buy bitcoins

Investors seeking to dabble in bitcoins will find it harder than they thought to get their hands on these invisible coins. You can't just wander down to your local bureau de change. This is because most financial institutions prefer not to accept credit card or PayPal payments for bitcoins, because these transactions can easily be reversed with a phone call to the card company, a process known as 'charge-backs'. Since it's hard to prove that any goods changed hands in the transfer of bitcoins, exchanges avoid this payment method and so do most private sellers.

At the moment, the main way to get your digital hands on bitcoins is through US outfits Coinbase and Circle, which offer purchases with credit cards, while Bittylicious, CoinCorner and Coinbase allow UK consumers to buy bitcoins using credit and debit cards on the Visa and MasterCard networks. A side point: physical bitcoins are just gimmicks – when you see pictures of gold coins emblazoned with a 'B', you're just looking at geek swag.

Insiders recommend that speculators instead buy bitcoins from reputable vendors or exchanges, or keep an eye on equity crowd-funding sites such as Seedrs and Bank of the Future, where bitcoin companies are increasingly going to fundraise. Make no mistake, backing a new bitcoin exchange carries a very high risk, but several bitcoin companies have chosen this route of entry because of the publicity and network growth it brings, and are doing well as a result – thus far.

Is it safe to hold bitcoins?

You've probably heard of one chap, James Howells, who threw away a hard drive with a wallet with 7,500 bitcoins on it, but on the whole, as long as you keep your wallet safe, your bitcoins will be safe too – as safe as cash would be in a real wallet. This is because of the blockchain, which tells the rest of the network what transactions have taken place.

Bitcoin 'nodes' use the blockchain to distinguish legitimate bitcoin transactions from attempts to re-spend coins that have already been spent elsewhere. Whenever a new block of transactions is created, it is added to the blockchain, creating an increasingly lengthy list of all the transactions that ever took place on the bitcoin network.

Bitcoin exchanges have proven slightly less secure. Any institution that holds a substantial amount of bitcoins becomes a target for hackers. In 2014, thieves stole $400 million from the most venerable bitcoin exchange, Mt Gox, which has struggled to rebuild its reputation.

More and more retailers, apps and even some of the new challenger banks are now accepting bitcoins because they believe that bitcoins have become an entrenched part of the digital payments landscape.

For those who don't actually want to hold the currency, bitcoin binary options is another way to dip your toe into the deep waters of bitcoin investing. This is high risk – you could also call this spread betting, as binary bets differ from traditional options in that you are not actually buying anything but rather just placing a side bet on an expected outcome. Trades are placed by predicting the direction an asset will move in during the specified time frame. The time that the option ends is called an expiry time. Expiry times range anywhere from 30 seconds until months away. At the end of the time, if the direction you chose was correct, you win the trade.

The blockchain and Ethereum

Blockchain, which is now commonly being referred to as Bitcoin 2.0, is in vogue. Many companies, from small technology start-ups to big banks, are experimenting with blockchain technology right now. It's estimated that more than $1 billion will be spent on blockchain by large financial institutions over the next 24 months.

Blockchain is a 'distributed ledger technology', a way to let companies make and verify transactions on a network instantaneously without a central authority. Think of blockchain as the elephant that never forgets. Every time a transaction takes place on the network, it is recorded. You can't go back and scrub out an entry – it's there for good. When the blockchain is changed, you can see all the tweaks along the way.

Why investors should care about blockchain

The focus on blockchain means that now could be the time to invest in other technologies based on the distributive ledger idea. This is where Ethereum comes in. It's a technology platform built on the same blockchain idea that powers Bitcoin – programmable money, but it is an open source project that allows the blockchain concept to be applied beyond financial transactions. This could result in blockchain-based contracts, blockchain-based businesses or whole other networks that have yet to be built. Skype co-founder Jaan Tallinn recently told me that he's hoping to use blockchain to solve huge environmental crises such as overfishing, deforestation and climate change. These ambitions may sound crazy, but quite a bit of cash is being ploughed into this industry, attracting investment from the likes of Barclays, Google, UBS and IBM. Some 42 banks have even joined forces in a new group, the R3 Consortium, which is experimenting with using blockchain for various applications, such as issuing bonds or trading shares or commodities.

Banks are particularly interested in using blockchain to send money to each other instantly and securely in the future – one of these technologies is called Ripple.

The rise of Ethereum

Ethereum is becoming a major cryptocurrency, but has yet to hit the mainstream – unlike bitcoin, which regularly makes headlines. Ethereum hit an all-time high of $17 in June, making it worth $1.3 billion in its first year of existence.

The thing to remember with any new currency or technology is that there are likely to be teething problems. In June 2016, Ethereum suffered a setback when the Decentralized Autonomous Organization (DAO), a system built on top of the coin, which acts like a digital venture capital fund, was drained of $53 million. Ethereum users were using the DAO to buy tokens – a bit like shares – which gave them voting powers on projects and investments, just as stockholders can help influence a company's strategy. In return, these investors would receive a share of the profits – it has been called 'the model for a new kind of decentralized corporation'.

As with Bitcoin, there are a number of sites and exchanges where you can purchase the coins (known as ether), but the most active exchange is poloniex.com, and you can also buy from retail outlets like bittylicious.com. Charlie Cox, a blockchain expert, tells me that several highly anticipated coins and tokens are to be released within the Ethereum framework, which will enable a wide variety of blockchain applications. He claims that there are a number of offerings in the pipeline that will utilize Ethereum's smart contracts and programmable money functionality, which could prove to be 'highly lucrative investments' when they are released as they are set to pave the way for an internet revolution. 'Think "early Google investor" kind of money if the gamble pays off – and it's not looking like a massive gamble currently as there is no viable competition to Ethereum they have not already absorbed', he says.

Other altcoins

Well over 1,500 altcoins have now been launched – although some have already been consigned to the history books. The majority have no real benefits over Bitcoin and most are just clones of older coins or are based on a gimmick or target audience such as Pizzacoin, Colacoin or Potcoin. While some might have a vaguely viable use case, most don't offer anything above and beyond Bitcoin, and therefore in the long run they are unlikely to survive. There are a few exceptions, however. The following coins have been picked out by insiders as ones to watch. Dash, formerly Darkcoin, is more anonymous than Bitcoin, with levels of security and cloaking that Bitcoin will never implement. It has seen steady growth of its network and price since inception. Litecoin is viewed as the silver to Bitcoin's gold, and although it looks like it's going to be knocked out of second place by Ethereum, it still has a substantial reach among cryptocurrency enthusiasts, as it enables considerably faster transaction times than Bitcoin. It tends to mimic Bitcoin's performance: when Bitcoin is doing well, generally speaking Litecoin is doing well, too.

And then there's Dogecoin, started as a joke and, based on an internet meme (Google it if you're a dog fan), given away in such large quantities in its early days that it created a massive and invested network of users. It was also the first coin to truly embrace social media, which enabled much of its syndication. For that reason, it has much viral success and a vast fan base, and is likely to be around for a while yet.

Carboncoin is attempting to offset the impact of all the electricity being wasted by the mining required to keep transactions running. It's removed all monetary incentives for people to mine the coin while at the same time lowering the computational power needed to keep the network transactions running. The entire network could be run off a couple of computers. Carboncoin has planted 2,500 trees to offset its initial mining period and has projects to plant over a million trees in Wyoming and large projects in the Amazon and China.

A new dawn of cryptocurrencies

With the advent of Ethereum and its rivals, Credits, Mastercoin and Coloured Coins, it will soon be much easier for individuals to create their own cryptocurrencies and tokens. There is a theory that the number of digital currencies could reach the hundreds of thousands within a few years, with uses ranging from corporate investment vehicles through to personal crowdfunding. Events and festivals, shops, theatres and cinemas could end up with their own currencies (making points and loyalty cards a thing of the past), right down to kids swapping personally created coins in their lunch break at school.

Spread betting

When you get to the heart of it, investing is much like gambling – you're weighing up the odds of making a decent return and trying to back a winner. This is why I'm including spread betting, which is just another way to gamble on the performance of the market – albeit one with a slightly sordid reputation.

Financial spread betting has become one of the most popular ways of trading in the UK because it allows traders to make a bet on a market without buying actual shares. At its most basic, a financial spread bet allows traders to bet on whether the value of something will rise or fall. This something could be a share in a company, an entire index, such as the FTSE 100, a currency or a commodity – even sports. Traders bet on the direction they think the price will move in, pledging an amount per point movement in price.

When you bet that the price will rise, this is known as going long, and when you reckon the price will fall, you are going short. In spread betting, there are two prices: the buy price, which is the price at which you can go long if you expect the market you're betting on to rise, and a sell price, which is the price at which you can go short if you expect the underlying market price to fall. The difference between the 'buy' price and 'sell' price is known as the spread. It's known as a bet because, like a bet at the bookies or down the races, you're exempt from Capital Gains Tax (CGT) on your winnings.

Losses can exceed deposits

Spread betting allows people on limited budgets to make bets on the market even when they couldn't necessarily afford to buy actual shares. The minimum bet can be as low as £2. Despite costing a relatively small amount of cash up front, the gains can be significant. But the risks are extremely high – this is another reason it's called betting. The more 'right' you are, the more you win. But the more wrong you are, the more you lose. You'll notice that ads from spread-betting companies now carry a warning: your losses may exceed your deposits.

Imagine that you are betting £10 on the FTSE 100 and you think it's likely to rise. You agree to 'buy' at 6,022 and the value of the index goes up by 100 points, to 6,122. At this point, you may decide to close your bet and 'sell', making 100 × £10, which is £1,000. Assume instead that you had a hunch that the FTSE 100 was likely to fall, chose to 'sell' at 6,022 and the FTSE fell by 100 points. If you closed your bet, you would still have made £1,000 because you guessed correctly.

Many people who get into spread betting see these numbers and immediately reach for their wallets, but check out what happens if you bet wrong. Let's take that original FTSE 100 example, where you've decided that the value of the index will definitely rise. But oh-oh, it actually falls by 100 points to 5,922. You decide to close the bet because you don't know how low the FTSE could fall. You are then forced to 'sell' at the lower price, which means you lose 100 × £10 per point, or £1,000. You will have the same loss if you short the market and it rises.

You can leave a spread bet running as long as you dare. You can close it after an hour if you've made a substantial gain, or leave the bet running – even when you've lost a lot of money – in the hope that the market will turn. Some spread-betting companies allow you to place a guaranteed 'stop loss' on your bet, which means you can limit your losses if the market goes against you – but you pay for this facility.

There are a number of spread-betting companies out there. Cantor Index, IG Index and City Index are some of the biggest. But don't be fooled by the City spin: this is gambling plain and simple; you are betting on an outcome against the bookmaker.

Contracts for difference

There is another financial product that is very similar to spread betting, and that's contracts for difference (CFDs). It's another way to bet on the performance of a company. If you have a hunch that the stock will go up or down, you can take out a contract with your CFD broker – it will pay you if you're right, but you pay them if you're wrong. Many investors fail to grasp that last part: they think that the cash they bet on the deal when the contract is created is all the money they'll lose – wrong. You can lose far more than your initial investment.

CFDs are a type of financial derivative, which just means that instead of buying an actual share, you're betting on the stock price movement. Let's take an example: you think that company XYZ is doing well, and predict that its stock will rise. You could buy some shares the old-fashioned way. Say each XYZ share was worth £10, so you bought 10 for £100 and the price rose to £15 – you've made £50, or £5 for each of your 10 shares.

The reason why investors might opt for a CFD instead is that you don't pay for the whole share: you just pay for a fraction of the share – this is known as the margin, and is usually between 10% and 20% of the value of the actual share. It's the same kind of deal as people get when they need a mortgage to buy a house – you put down a deposit.

If we imagine that the margin is 20%, that same £100 would let you bet against 50 of the same XYZ shares. It's a leveraged transaction, or in layman's terms, a way to borrow to gamble. If XYZ's share price rises to £15, as before, you make £250 profit instead of just £50. There are dealing costs, so you won't take home the whole amount. If XYZ's shares fall to £5 instead, you've lost £250, so you owe the broker another £150. Once you start losing, you'll start receiving the dreaded margins calls – requests from your broker to deposit further cash to cover your losses.

It's worth remembering that CFDs were created in the eighties as a way for traders to hedge their bets on stock that they actually owned. These nifty products allowed City institutions that were holding XYZ stock to profit from short-term falls in price by shorting it – but to hang on to the real stock, believing it would rise in the long term. CFDs were made available to UK retail investors in the late nineties, but have a bad rap because many inexperienced people have lost a lot of money. As with options trading, you can pay for a stop loss to minimize the amount that you can lose.

Unlike spread betting, CFDs are not exempt from CGT, but only from stamp duty. You have to pay stamp duty on actual shares. If you want to find a CFD broker, there are lists of the top brokers online, but proceed with caution – losses can be unlimited if the market goes against you.

Start-ups

The one thing that I've learnt over a decade of writing about business is that the perceived value of something is achieved through this equation: $V = M + E$, or Value equals Maths plus Emotion. Never underestimate the role of market sentiment in giving a company value – or taking it away. This is how some start-ups can go for years, achieving billion-pound valuations, without turning a profit or even having any decent sales. People look at its financial ambitions, achievements and management and have an emotional response; they believe it will be successful. I say this because backing start-ups is a tricky business and none of us is infallible. Whenever you're trying to ascertain the value of a start-up, some emotion has been mixed in there at some point. The question you need to ask is: has that emotion caused the investment to be overvalued or undervalued? With that note of caution out of the way, start-ups are a high-risk, high-reward investment.

Equity crowdfunding

Crowdfunding, in various forms, has been around for centuries. At its most basic, crowdfunding just means tapping up friends and fans for small sums of cash to make a project happen. The model was formalized by the creation of platforms where these contributions could be logged, rewards explained, and transparency given to the whole process.

Crowdfunding comes in several different guises. There are donations, which means what it has always meant and is no different from the old church collecting plate. This is the model used by the platforms collecting cash for charity, such as JustGiving. Then there is rewards-based crowdfunding, where pledges are exchanged for the promise of goods or services down the line. This is the model you find on Kickstarter, for example.

Many investors confuse Kickstarter pledges with pre-orders. The reality is that you may never get your hands on the drone or smartwatch that you back. You're putting up your cash to help a venture succeed and, if it does, you share in the rewards.

Then there's equity-based crowdfunding, whereby growing companies exchange shares for growth capital. This model was pioneered in the UK by Crowdcube, which launched in 2011, and Seedrs, which came to market slightly later. This has become an increasingly popular way for early-stage firms to raise finance, especially after small-business lending became less attractive to banks in the wake of the financial crisis. Lastly, there is debt crowdfunding – or peer-to-peer – which is covered in an earlier chapter.

Donations and rewards-based crowdfunding aren't much use to investors – the first is classic philanthropy and the latter is glorified shopping – but equity-based crowdfunding is becoming quite the phenomenon.

There are major risks

Equity crowdfunding is still a very young industry. It took off at the tail end of a financial crisis but has yet to be tested by one. It's also so new that only a handful of businesses that have received financing through equity crowdfunding have exited. The Camden Town Brewery is one notable success story: it was sold for around £85 million to drinks giant AB InBev, owner of Budweiser, Stella Artois and Beck's, in December 2015 and the armchair investors who backed it on Crowdcube received 'a multiple return'. E-Car Club, the electric car sharing scheme, was another significant exit, with the 63 investors who backed it in 2013 being handed around three times their money back. Investors in E-Car Club put in an average of £1,500 apiece. The UK's biggest crowdfunding failure to date was revealed in February 2016. Rebus, a claims management company, went bust after raising more than £800,000 from 100 investors on Crowdcube. One investor lost £135,000 on that single deal. The company has since been accused of misleading practices.

Having such a small pool of success stories means that we still don't really know what the average returns for investors will look like. How do you draw an average from a handful of companies?

The whole asset class has surged in popularity in an environment of low interest rates, where investors have become increasingly desperate to make decent returns on their money. There's a hell of a lot of hype in the market, with investors going for volume plays, backing loads of start-ups in the hopes of rewards down the line. They may get those rewards or they may lose their money – we just don't know.

Betting on early-stage companies is always risky. How can you know if that business will be around in five or ten years? It's impossible to predict how markets or demand will change down the line. And lest we forget, half of all start-ups fail within the first five years. A recent report by AltFi Data and the law firm Nabarro, which looked at the industry as a whole, found that one in five companies that raised money on equity crowdfunding platforms between 2011 and 2013 went bankrupt. The Financial Conduct Authority (FCA) has also warned that investors should expect between 50% and 70% of their investments to fail.

The flipside

Crowdfunding is a godsend for the start-ups themselves. It's a way to raise money, and lock in future customers, in one fell swoop. Here's why. Imagine you find a great beer made by an independent brewery, let's call it Hops Ltd. That company is crowdfunding and you think, 'I love the beer, I want these guys to succeed', so you back the campaign. What happens next? Every time you see a Hops Ltd beer on tap, you'll order it. You have a vested interest in the brewery's survival. You'll tell your friends about it, you'll read articles about its progress – you've become a card-carrying devotee.

One of the major criticisms of the sector is that valuations can be very high, and are often predicated on future success rather than on profits today. Does this mean that investors are being taken for a ride? Valuations are notoriously subjective, and around nine out of ten companies that choose to raise money through crowdfunding are pre-profit or have no trading history, according to equity platform Growthdeck, so there's no straightforward answer. Remember that old cliché when weighing up a crowdfunded deal: a business is only worth what someone is willing to pay for it.

There are hundreds of crowdfunding platforms out there, and the growth in the sector is undeniable. Crowdcube more than doubled its number of active investors to 250,000 in 2015, with £85 million invested across the year.

Crowdfunding: the basics

Most platforms will let armchair investors back a company with as little as £10. The company has to hit its target in order to get a penny of the funds raised. If it falls short, the money is returned to investors. The platform takes a fee – up to 7% is standard, including charges – and then the business has to crack on and hit its targets.

Remember that investors can only make their returns once that company is sold, lists on the stock market or buys their shares back. This could take many years or never happen at all. If you want to exit your investment, you may struggle, as there's no secondary market on which to find buyers for your shares.

The company you're seeking to back should have an exit strategy in place, which it will detail in its prospectus. Never back a company without checking out the financials. The crowdfunding platforms – the reputable ones anyway – do a significant amount of due diligence, but ultimately, it's a case of caveat emptor.

Unlike traditional equities, you're unlikely to receive dividends from the company you help to crowdfund. Start-ups don't usually make enough profit to pay out to shareholders in this way. There is also the danger that your shareholding will be diluted in future rounds. This is known as 'dilution risk' and happens when the start-up issues more shares to raise more money down the line, reducing the value of your investment.

It is not recommended to invest more than 10% of your investable wealth in crowdfunding. There has been some implicit support of the sector from the government, which has included it in its Innovative Finance Isa, alongside peer-to-peer, and made some crowdfunded investments eligible for special tax reliefs under the Enterprise Investment Scheme (EIS) or Seed Enterprise Investment Scheme (SEIS) rules. More on EIS in the next section.

One final point: the UK crowdfunding landscape became a little more interesting in 2016 after the latest tweak to the Jobs Act came into force on 16 May, allowing US investors to back crowdfunding campaigns in the UK for the first time. Whether this will create a surge of demand, possibly driving up valuations even further, remains to be seen.

Angel investing and the Enterprise Investment Scheme

The problem with angel investing is that it sounds very glamorous. In some ways, it is. You become the financial archangel Gabriel, bestowing your monies like manna from heaven upon the devoted faithful entrepreneurs who stake their souls on their success. Some successful angels have turned into pseudo-rock stars, with huge followings on social media and start-up founders hanging on their every word. But the reality of angel investing, or so I'm told, is tough. You have to have an extraordinary network in order to hear about the best companies to invest in, or be part of a syndicate. Most of the companies you back will go bust, which can take a toll on your confidence – especially where you have devoted a lot of time to helping that business to grow. You must rely on just one or two big winners to make your money – if, indeed, you have any at all.

Unlike the United States, where angel investors must prove they have sufficient income to start backing early-stage companies, and get formal accreditation, anyone can be an angel investor in this country. Under the FCA rules, individual private investors in the UK must be 'high net worth' or 'sophisticated', but this is a box-ticking exercise – it's all done through self-certification. This means that the angel industry is booming. In 2015, over 1 million angel investors backed small businesses across the UK, according to the UK Business Angels Association.

The Enterprise Investment Scheme

The other reason that angel investing is thriving in the UK is because of a little initiative called the Enterprise Investment Scheme. The amount of capital raised through EIS between 2014 and 2015 hit a record high, topping £1.7 billion, according to HMRC data. The number of companies accessing capital through this vehicle rose from 2,800 to 3,130 from 2013 to 2014, and is heading for another record year. Since EIS was created in 1993, almost 25,000 businesses have received more than £14 billion of funding from the scheme.

EIS incentivizes angel investors to back early-stage, risky companies by offering 30% Income Tax relief up to a maximum of £1 million a year. There is no minimum investment, and if shares are held for at least three years, any profits from their sale are free from CGT. There are lots of rules governing eligibility: you can't be a director or employee of the company to benefit; you can't even be related to the founder.

There is also a 'carry back' facility, which allows all or part of the cost of shares acquired in one tax year to be treated as though those shares had been acquired in the preceding tax year. This means that you can actually purchase £2 million worth of EIS shares in the current tax year but carry back £1 million to the one before.

EIS has a sister scheme, the Seed Enterprise Investment Scheme, which is aimed at even smaller, far riskier companies. It offers even higher Income Tax relief, at 50%, but for investments capped at £100,000 a year. Again, you'll need to hold on to those shares for three years at a minimum.

Should you become an angel investor?

Before you think about how to become an angel investor, you need to consider whether you should. How much money can you afford to lose? That is the amount that you should set aside for this endeavour, and no more. How much time can you spend on your investment companies? Bear in mind that before you've given away a penny, you'll have to spend a decent chunk of time poring over business plans and financial results. It is estimated that to make a proper evaluation, an angel must spend 20 hours, on average, looking through a company's financials.

You do really need deep pockets to stand a chance of making money. Angel investors advise investing in a diversified portfolio of start-ups, and making peace with the fact that most will fail from the off. You need to have enough money to make those early-stage seed investments, but to make big returns out of the super-successful companies, you'll need to have even more money to invest in follow-on rounds. Tripling down on the one company that makes it to the big time – and this could be 1 in 20 start-ups – is how you will most likely make all your money.

This is why many would-be angels elect to join an angel syndicate. There is typically a lead angel investor, or flock of angels, who will decide which companies to back, and find opportunities. The crowd then piles in behind them.

The upside of being part of a syndicate is that it helps spread risk; each investor is only stumping up a small portion of the total pot.

You pay to play, and in return for the great tip, the lead investor will take a 'carry fee', which means he or she will take a larger slice of the profits down the line. For most syndicates, you'll need to have £30,000–£40,000 ready to invest, either in one go, or broken down into smaller chunks and invested in a series of companies.

Starting your own business

Here's a really crazy notion: use your savings to start your own business. This only applies to people who have a start-up idea already, but if you have the entrepreneurial inclination, this could be an interesting use for your capital. It's a way of ensuring that you, and you alone, generate the maximum return from your skills, expertise and money.

Starting a business is extremely risky. Half of all start-ups fail within the first five years, and if you go bankrupt, there will be no way to salvage any of your initial investment in the business. But compared to other investments, none will ever be as transparent as the one you make yourself. You know how hard you are prepared to work to get the business off the ground, you know your limits, and you should know your market.

You could say that starting a business is the ultimate passion investment. It will take up a significant chunk of your time, and to be successful, you will need to be completely obsessed. You may not reap the rewards for many years – some start-up founders flip their businesses within months, but this is rare; it usually takes time to build value in a company.

People start businesses for two reasons: they've spotted a gap in the market and they have a clever idea to meet this demand, or they are doing something that's already been done, but think they can do it better than the competition. Whichever camp you fall into, it may be useful to look at the costs involved in building a new company.

According to a recent study commissioned by Geniac, an online business service, the average UK start-up spends £22,756 in its first year. This figure takes into account incorporation costs, accountants' fees, some legal costs, HR overheads and general administration.

It does not include the money spent on business-specific activities, such as buying stock or developing a product.

The biggest overhead, according to the business owners questioned for the survey, was legal costs, followed by all the costs of actually forming the company.

The definition of an investment is the action whereby you put money into an endeavour with the purpose of making additional income or profit. This is one of the principal reasons that entrepreneurs start businesses, so bears including in this section.

A start-up as an investment

As with any investment, you should never bet all your savings on your business idea. There are other ways to raise start-up capital: low-interest credit cards have been used by many British entrepreneurs to get through their first few months in business, while crowd-funding is becoming an increasingly popular avenue for raising growth capital from fans and friends.

If you're struggling to come up with a killer business idea, you might want to consider buying a franchise. Franchising is a model that allows brands to expand by outsourcing new outlets to entrepreneurs. These people become self-employed franchisees, but benefit from a well-established name and access to ongoing sales and marketing support.

It's proved a successful model for many wannabe business owners. According to the British Franchise Association, four in five new franchises are profitable within two years. There are now more than 44,000 franchisee-owned outlets in the UK, a rise of 17% since the 2008 recession.

Retired workers can now dip into their pension pots for start-up capital. The pension freedoms introduced in April 2014 have allowed over-55s access to their pension savings, but this may not be the most tax-efficient way to draw down those funds. Pension-led funding, whereby money is borrowed from the pension but repaid back into the same pot, with interest, is generally seen as a much safer way of accessing your retirement nest egg.

Starting a business may be risky, but when weighed up against some of the other options at this end of the book, perhaps not that risky by comparison. You should apply the same level of due diligence to an investment in yourself as you would to any other kind of investment.

Conclusion

You've now learnt the basics about some of the riskiest investments available to people seeking high returns. These are the punts one should only make with money one can afford to lose. In some cases, such as with spread betting, we're talking glorified gambling – or actual gambling, according to UK law. It is actually illegal in the United States, Japan and Australia. The purpose of including CFDs and spread betting in this chapter was not to promote them as worthwhile uses for your money, but to explain how they work. An educated investor is an empowered investor. People are much more likely to lose money when they dabble in investments or financial products that they don't understand.

The riskier the investment, the more important it becomes that the investor is able to admit, 'I was wrong'. It is only by accepting the issue and cutting your losses that you can move on. Human beings don't like being wrong, and this can create what's known as 'cognitive dissonance'. This is when two statements, such as 'I'm a good investor' and 'This was a poor investment decision', struggle to co-exist in the mind. It's this battle between these two perceptions that causes investors to hold on to losing positions too long, or to throw good money after bad. To avoid the pain of admitting culpability, investors will often look for a scapegoat. Having someone to blame has a positive outcome, however, as it tends to accelerate the speed at which the investor gets out of the investment: 'You sent me down the wrong path so I'm going to get out of this mess as fast as I can', as opposed to, 'I'm a good investor but this has gone wrong; it will probably be okay if I wait a while longer'.

Understanding the psychology of investing is important, because we don't make the best decisions when we are ruled by emotion.

The ones that got away 07

There are a few investments that haven't been included in this book for a variety of reasons. It could be because the market is extremely illiquid, making it very difficult to get involved, and I've chosen not to dangle the impossible. There are also more esoteric investments that I would rather avoid, either because experts have warned me that many retail investors have lost a lot of money, or because the complexity and capital minimums required to play in that space mean it's probably best left to the professionals.

Too risky

Derivatives and structured products have a bad name because several banks got into a lot of trouble in recent years when it was discovered they had sold unnecessarily complex products to small businesses that didn't really understand what they were buying. The more vanilla derivatives, futures and options, based on well-known stocks, are discussed earlier in the book, but the weird ones are to be avoided. Any derivative that is offered by a bank, where you're reliant on that same bank to name the price to get out of it, is toxic. This is an illiquid market and by the time you turn around and want out of the deal, the bank could decide that it wants a massive bung to let you go.

Heed the words of Peter Lynch, the investor emeritus. He managed the Fidelity Magellan Fund from 1977 to 1990, driving up the fund's assets from $20 million to $14 billion. His advice: 'Never invest in any idea you can't illustrate with a crayon.'

Another risky field is land banking. This is where an investor buys a plot of land that hasn't been granted planning permission, usually through a land-banking scheme. It's a real gamble as there's no guarantee that planning will ever be granted. The value of the land is only unlocked once it is sold, so your money is inaccessible until a buyer is found. Schemes may promise that you will double or even quadruple your investment, but there's rarely any evidence that this will definitely be the case.

Many land-banking schemes have left investors out of pocket, either because the plot was too small to build on or because it is classed as green-belt land, which prevents developers throwing up tower blocks. This is also an unregulated area and there are many scams out there – watch out for unsolicited e-mails making far-fetched promises about foreign lands of plenty.

Also at the riskier end of the investment spectrum, there are serious returns to be made from investing in early-stage companies. There are several ways to do this, from angel investing to funds focusing on small-caps. Venture capital trusts, or VCTs, have not been included in this book. This is because this is not investing, per se. It's a tax wrapper: a way to save 30% on your Income Tax by putting a maximum of £200,000 into a group of growing firms for a minimum of five years. Many of the VCTs out there serve that sole purpose. The money is parked in these small companies, generating the tax break for the investor. If the start-ups that receive the growth capital do spectacularly well and sell for a huge sum, some VCT firms even limit the benefit to the investor to that tax break alone; the massive return is pocketed by the VCT operator. Some do share the spoils, but the main incentive here is so-called 'tax efficiency', which is what tax avoidance is called when it's approved by HMRC.

Too illiquid

Classic board games may be rising in value rapidly, but few people will stumble upon an original version of Monopoly (one sold for £90,000 in 2015) in mint condition, in their attic.

Similarly, some old toy pedal cars have soared in value in recent years, prompting experts to warn that many Brits could be unwittingly leaving a strong investment rotting in their shed. The old Austin J40 pedal car, which was made by the car company Austin from 1949 to 1971, is worth 'thousands', apparently. Rusting, missing wheels or dented, that estimate falls to 'many hundreds of pounds', but collectors are still keen to snap up rust-buckets with the aim of doing them up, or using them for parts. But the truth is that this market is tiny and niche. Yes, a 1956 Pontiac Club de Mer concept pedal car recently sold in the United States for nearly $34,000, but it's unlikely that you'll find one of these in your garage. Just in case you are reading this and thinking, 'We have an old Noddy car out the back', that could be worth as much as £100, while 1990s battery-powered ride-on cars such as Jaguars may also be valuable. David Jinks, a collectables expert and former editor of *Model Price Guide*, also claimed that typical Tri-ang doll's prams from the 1960s can fetch up to £100, and the Rolls-Royce of doll's prams, the Silver Cross, can achieve £200 or more.

Cufflinks and tie pins have become popular collectables, especially among City types. But there are few specialist dealers in these sectors, and very little data to show how fast these assets are appreciating. Anecdotally, it appears that sixties and seventies cufflinks are particularly popular. Searches on eBay show that some of the retro beauties made by Van Cleef & Arpels, featuring precious and semi-precious stones, were listed for as much as £5,000.

Pinball machines, while niche, can prove savvy investments, but usually only when bought damaged or through a distressed sale. Trawling through pinball forums, there are countless warnings that rookies are more likely to lose money than make it, but, for argument's sake, let's look at the potential earnings. One collector, who picked up a 1994 Twilight Zone – out of all the retro pinball machines, those released in the eighties or nineties are the most desirable – for $2,600, claims that just two years later it was worth $5,000. But what's really great about pinball machines is that once you find a home for them – perhaps in a local bar or arcade, they pay dividends in the form of 50p coins from punters who play the game.

Most of the people who claim they have made big bucks from trading pinball machines are experts, capable of fixing broken ramps, lamps and optical switches ('optos', to those in the know). They are also the people who will end up buying your clapped-out machine for a song once you make a few wrong turns with the repairs, so of course they want ignorant investors to pile in.

Rugs and carpets used to be a rather fun – if niche – investment, but these have unravelled in recent years. According to the Coutts Passion Index, in 2015 this was one of the worst performers out of all the hobby investments, posting growth of just 1%, compared to an average of 7% growth per year from 2005 to 2014. Rugs and carpets are awkward to store and you need an expert to value the things – and a few unwanted moths could completely destroy your investment, so floor coverings have been left out.

There are many different hobby or passion investments out there: collectables that tend to appreciate in value. I have included some, such as classic cars and stamps, but have not included rare coins or rare books. This may seem unfair, as all of these different investment avenues require a significant level of research, a vast network of contacts to source the things, and all are illiquid – you can't be sure of finding a buyer when you want one, or getting the price that you would consider fair. The reason why I have included classic cars is as more of a cautionary tale, and because it's one of the best-performing passion investments out there.

Just in case you're a bibliophile, know that first editions – only of the most sought-after fiction – have increased in value by around 400% over the past 10 years. The most valuable book is F Scott Fitzgerald's *The Great Gatsby* from 1925, which was valued at £246,636 in 2015. *The Hobbit* by J R R Tolkien was the second most valuable book in the same index, published by Stanley Gibbons Investments, which specializes in tangible assets, at £65,420.

If you own one of just 500 first editions of J K Rowling's *Harry Potter and the Philosopher's Stone*, your £10.99 investment could be worth as much as £17,000 now. Children's classics are also a lucrative niche, when they are in good condition, especially when illustrated.

If you're interested in rare coins, these are defined as coins of which there are only a few hundred at a maximum, minted before 1933.

Numismatics, or the collection of currency, is highly complex and opaque – most deals take place privately, so the returns are unknown.

Plain dodgy

Beanie babies are a collectable that we've avoided like the plague. These plush toys were once the investors' darling, with some rare ones changing hands for as much as $5,000 in the late nineties. Beanie Babies, the company, recorded sales of $1.4 billion in 1998. But if you want to hear a cautionary tale that explains why you should never put all your money into one thing, watch Chris Robinson's documentary entitled *Bankrupt By Beanies*, which tells the story of how his family invested $100,000 in the fluffy, colourful toys, only to lose it all when demand fell off a cliff.

Every year there seems to be an investment expert or website claiming that VHS is making a comeback as a collectable. It's never really materialized, although there are some highly valuable old videos out there – usually old horror films. But before you dig out your dog-eared collection of tapes from the attic, the list is pretty small. Reliable gems are: *Satan War* (1979), *The Beast in Heat* (1977) and *Lemora, Lady Dracula* (1973), which now all trade for more than $1,000.

Conclusion
That's a wrap

Hopefully, whether you're just starting to build a portfolio or looking to further diversify your investments, this has been a useful read. Each different asset class warrants a book in its own right, so this has been a taster of the range of possibilities on offer to the retail investor.

If you are to take anything away from this book, let it be these three things: diversification is crucial; always check fees and charges; and try to avoid the twin demons of fear and greed.

On diversification, even experienced investors try not to put all their eggs in one basket. You need to make sure that your portfolio spans many different industries, geographies and asset classes, and that you have a mix of securities that do well in the good times, but also a few that perform well in tougher economic conditions.

Fees – especially hidden fees – can decimate your returns. Remember that this is how the brokers and investment managers make their money – and those City skyscrapers don't come cheap.

Knowledge is power

The aim of this book has been to simplify some of the concepts and the terminology used in the investment world. Remember that when you're selling a service, as all these City institutions are, it is in their best interests to make the thing they are selling as mysterious and opaque as possible. We will always pay more for something that we think is too complicated for us to grasp. Now that you have grasped the fundamentals of investing, macroeconomics and the vicissitudes of the global markets should become more interesting. Keep an eye on the performance of sterling, the creep of inflation, and the highs and lows of other market economies.

The financial markets have been the preserve of the few for a long time. It is only just now going through a process of genuine democratization so that all of us can have a go at making more from our money. Always demand to hear your options explained in plain English, ask about what you stand to lose, and work out the impact of that wonder of the world – compound interest – on your returns. Remember that compound interest giveth with one hand, so if you reinvest your gains you will make more money, but also taketh away, as those innocent-seeming 1–2% management fees morph into huge pay-outs.

You will never regret spending a little more time investigating the pros and cons of each investment. As Benjamin Franklin, one of the founding fathers of the United States, famously said: 'An investment in knowledge pays the best interest.' This is a man who grew up with nothing, but became a self-made man by investing in what he knew and understood.

Investing is not a hard science. Unlike chemistry or maths, doing the same thing over and over is not guaranteed to generate the same result. Your investment strategies must evolve as markets change.

Be cold. Be hard. Be calculated

Investing should not be an emotional pastime. Life has plenty of highs and lows already, without using your hard-earned cash to give you thrills. If the move you're planning to make gives you a rush of adrenaline and makes you feel giddy, don't do it. Your decisions need to be cold, calculated and well thought through. If you play the money markets like you're in a casino, the house will always win. Never forget that it is estimated that only 6–10% of investors ever reach their financial goals – make sure you're the one in ten.

Take the time to understand what you're investing in and why. Famous investor Peter Lynch puts it well: 'Although it's easy to forget sometimes, a share is not a lottery ticket... it's part-ownership of a business.' You don't need to try to get your head around every single asset class; you just need to pick a few to understand well.

Smart investors are very good at managing their emotions at all times, especially in extraordinary circumstances. The reason that bull and bear markets exist is because human beings are fallible, and apt to follow each other blindly, even if it's to their mutual destruction. In fact, when people are running scared, that can be a very good buying opportunity – if you're making a long-term play, which most of you should be. Sometimes the markets are scared witless for good reason, and you shouldn't be a contrarian just for the sake of it, but don't be afraid to go against the tide. As Warren Buffet once said: 'We simply attempt to be fearful when others are greedy and to be greedy only when others are fearful.'

Where there's muck there's brass

Don't discount markets that seem boring, or a bit grubby. Not all your investments have to pass the 'dinner party' test – we may not like talking about sewage companies but we should never forget to be grateful that they are there. The old saying goes that where there's muck there's brass, and it's certainly true that investors are frequently taken in by rising stars, with exciting new technologies and big ideas, and can forget about the companies that are simply required to keep the world clean and safe. 'Generally, the greater the stigma or revulsion, the better the bargain' is the oft-quoted advice from billionaire Seth Klarman.

The aim of investing is to create more wealth from your hard-earned capital, accepting a level of risk that works for you. Each individual's risk tolerance is different, and much will depend on how much money you have to invest and how much you can afford to lose. This is why listening to advice from friends and colleagues can be misleading. There is no one right way to invest, otherwise everyone would be doing it.

You may be wondering how best to amplify the £40,000 you've saved over your lifetime, while your friend may be wondering how to invest the £500,000 he or she was bequeathed in a relative's will. You can see how the emotion attached to these two sets of circumstances would be different, and why the investment strategy would be equally different. I love a Warren Buffet quote as much as the next person, but we must never forget that he is a billionaire – if he makes a few mistakes, he'll still be a billionaire. That's a pretty nice safety net.

Good luck and happy investing.

GLOSSARY

'A' shares Most companies will have just one class of share: ordinary shares. But as they grow, raise money and begin doling out shares to investors, they may start to issue different share classes. This allows the company to vary the dividends paid to different shareholders, and to create non-voting shares and/or bespoke shares for employees or family members. 'A' shares are ordinary shares that typically carry fewer or no votes, but they usually carry more votes than 'B' shares.

absolute return Investments designed to deliver positive returns regardless of the investment environment. However, nothing is ever certain, and absolute return funds rarely live up to their promises.

accumulation Some funds will offer investors the option to reinvest their income from the fund – usually the dividend – as they are paid out. This helps boost your final pot through the magic of compounding.

actively managed fund Unlike funds that passively track an index, an actively managed fund employs a professional investment manager to pick the stocks they believe will outperform the market. These funds aim to outperform passive investments and are usually fiercely competitive, trying to beat peers, too.

activist Activists don't just come in the tree-hugging variety. Activist investors – often from hedge funds – will buy enough shares in a company to give them rights over how it's managed. They then push through changes that they believe will increase the value of their investment, such as raising dividends or selling off valuable assets.

administration This is not a word that any investor wants to see. When a company is distressed and unlikely to survive, the administrators are called in to either try to help the company avoid administration or to liquidate the assets fairly so that creditors aren't left completely high and dry.

affirmative covenant An affirmative covenant is a type of promise or contract that requires a party to commit to a course of action. In bonds, this may be a pledge by the issuer to insure the bond, or promise that it will pay regular dividends. A negative covenant is a promise not to do something, such as sell certain assets.

all-gilt index An index made up solely of UK government bonds.

alternative investment Many of the investment options discussed in this book are alternative investments. These fall outside the scope of equities, bonds and commodities, and can be anything from art to crowdfunding.

Alternative Investment Market (AIM) The stock market operated by the London Stock Exchange that focuses on smaller companies. The AIM market has much lighter regulation than the main market, which means it's less expensive to list. Since its launch in 1995, over 3,600 companies have joined AIM.

amortization You usually come across this word when companies talk about profits in EBITDA terms (earnings before interest, tax, depreciation and amortization). Amortization means the fall in value of the company's intangible assets, such as intellectual property.

angel investor A wealthy individual who backs early-stage companies, typically investing between £10,000 and £250,000 a pop.

annual general meeting (AGM) Each year, a limited company must hold an annual general meeting to give shareholders the opportunity to hold management to account over decisions that have been made, and to ask questions about the future of the business. All shareholders are entitled to attend and vote on proposals, such as bigger pay packets for the chief executive.

annualized return The total return from an investment, broken down into a yearly amount. This figure can disguise volatility, as it hides the peaks and troughs.

annual management charge The fee charged by fund managers to run a fund. This averages out to about 0.75% across most actively managed funds.

annuity A fixed sum of money paid to someone each year, for a prolonged period of time. Not to be confused with the annuity in the insurance world, which can be paid out in a lump sum.

arbitrage This is how investors profit from minute market differences, buying an instrument in one and simultaneously selling in another, making a profit in the process. An example is if there are two fruit markets near you and one is selling oranges for 10p each and the other is selling them for 20p each; if you buy at 10p and sell at 20p, you pocket the 10p difference.

ask price The price at which an investor is willing to sell a security.

asset This is an item with value. When talking about investments, we mean a share, a bond, an option, a commodity and so on. Assets can be tangible – physically exist – or be intangible, such as a brand or intellectual property.

asset class The type of asset. The three main asset classes are equities, bonds and financial instruments.

auditor An official whose job it is to check the accuracy of company accounts and records carefully, and flag any anomalies.

balance sheet A balance sheet is a financial report summarizing all of a company's assets, liabilities and equity as of a given point in time. It is typically used to estimate a company's financial health – when liabilities start to overwhelm the assets, you're in trouble.

Bank of England The Bank of England is the UK's central bank, and issues the nation's currency, sets interest rates and oversees wider monetary policy – it can print imaginary money to prop up the economy when required, through quantitative easing.

bankruptcy When a company or individual is overwhelmed by debt, they can declare bankruptcy, which gives creditors the chance to get some of their money back through the liquidation of available assets, while forgiving the remainder of the debt.

base rate This is the interest rate set by the Bank of England.

basis point One basis point is equivalent to 1/100th of 1%. It is used to describe changes in interest rates and bond yields. If a bond yield rises from 4.00% to 4.50%, that's an increase of 50 basis points.

bear An investor who believes prices will fall.

bear fund A mutual fund designed to provide returns when the market's value drops.

bear market Beware the bear. A bear market comes about when the prices of securities fall, creating a mood of pessimism and causing investors to sell out their positions, which then drives prices down even further. It's named after the bear because the animal typically swipes its claws down. The opposite of a bear market is a bull market.

benchmark index A benchmark index gives the investor a point of reference for evaluating a fund's performance. For example, if your fund manager had built a portfolio of energy-related stocks, you could compare it to the wider energy index to see whether he or she has beaten the market.

bid–offer spread Also known as the bid–ask or buy–sell spread, this is the difference in price between the highest price that a buyer is willing to pay for something and the lowest price for which a seller is willing to sell that thing.

bid price The bid price is the amount that a buyer is willing to pay for a security. The opposite of the bid price is the ask price, which is the price a seller wants to receive for his or her shares.

bid size the number of shares an investor is willing to purchase at the bid price.

bid yield The bid yield is the return to the investor. This number is arrived at by looking at the bid price, the coupon rate and the time remaining to maturity.

binary bet Binary bets allow traders to gamble on the performance of a range of securities. Unlike spread betting, where losses are unlimited, with binary betting you cannot lose more than you bet.

blue chip A blue chip is a company that is generally seen to be financially sound, well established and trustworthy. These tend to be household names and perform consistently well, even through downturns. Fun fact: the name 'blue chip' originates from poker. The blue chips are the ones with the highest value.

bond Bonds are commonly referred to as fixed-income securities because they pay the bondholder interest – or coupons – at regular intervals. They are a form of debt, used by companies and governments to raise money.

bottom line The bottom line is a company's net profits. It's called the bottom line because it is usually found right at the bottom of the income statement: it's the profit figure that is reached after taking out taxes, interest and other considerations. Companies that improve their bottom line do so by increasing revenues or cutting costs.

broker or brokerage This is the middleman who helps investors to buy or sell securities, taking a fee for their trouble.

bubble A bubble is formed when prices surge rapidly and are deemed to be overinflated. The most famous bubble in recent times was the dotcom boom in the nineties, when investors were ploughing huge sums into expensive tech stocks, only to lose everything when the market crashed. Bubbles have a tendency to burst.

bull An investor who believes prices will rise.

bull market A market in which prices are rising, creating a mood of optimism, which then encourages traders to keep buying, forcing prices still higher. It's called a bull market because a bull thrusts its horns up into the air. The opposite of a bull market is a bear market.

bulldog A bulldog bond is a bond issued in the UK by foreign investors seeking exposure to the pound sterling. A bulldog market is the name given to the internal market filled with foreign bonds issued in the UK. The bulldog is, of course, the national symbol for Britain.

call auction or call market This takes place on an exchange. It's when a buyer, who has set a maximum price he or she is willing to pay for a security, and a seller, who has set the minimum price he or she is willing to accept, are matched. Think of this like Match.com, but for trades.

call option A call option gives an investor the right, but not the obligation, to buy a stock, bond, commodity or other instrument at an agreed price within a specific time frame. Used in options trading, you use a call option when you want the price of the underlying asset to increase, generating a profit (because you can buy and then instantly sell, pocketing the difference). See also *put option*.

cap The highest point to which a rate or charge can rise.

capital This refers either to cold, hard cash, or to the value of certain assets.

capital gain Capital gain is made when an asset is sold for more than it was bought for.

Capital Gains Tax (CGT) Capital Gains Tax is the tax you pay on the profit generated when you sell something that's increased in value. You are taxed only on the gain, not the full amount of money you receive for the sale.

capital market Capital markets are the markets where equity and debt instruments, such as equities and bonds, are bought and sold, such as the London Stock Exchange.

cash flow Cash is king, or so they say. Cash flow measures the money flowing in and out of a business, and represents the available cash on hand. Positive cash flow means there's enough money in the bank to settle debts and reinvest into the business, whereas negative cash flow usually means there's trouble ahead; if debts considerably outweigh cash, the company could slip into insolvency. Not to be confused with revenue, which is the money generated by a business in sales, but which doesn't necessarily refer to the actual amount of money held by the business.

chief executive officer (CEO) The boss.

chief financial officer (CFO) The financial brains of the operation and – usually – the person who holds the purse strings.

Chinese wall Companies use Chinese walls to avoid conflict of interest. The wall is metaphorically erected between two teams that have information that could affect each other, such as investment banks, which may be advising client A on how to grow the business but also representing company B, which wants to launch a hostile takeover against A.

City of London Also known simply as 'the City' or 'the square mile', this is the area around and to the east of St Paul's Cathedral in London, comprising banks, brokerages, insurance firms, trading houses and other financial institutions.

clearing house Futures exchanges all have their own clearing houses. This is where the total amounts of money owed by the buyers and sellers are totted up at the end of each trading session. The clearing house will have a minimum sum of money it is required to hold against all the futures that are in play.

closed-ended fund A closed-ended fund is created by raising a specified amount of money through an initial public offering, selling a set number of shares to investors. It is traded like a public company. Unlike open-ended funds, new shares can't just be created to meet demand. The fund is actively managed by an investment adviser and usually focuses on a specific niche, such as emerging markets or precious metals.

commission The cut that brokers or investment advisers take from each deal they handle.

commodity Commodities are products that are generic, such as crude oil, grains or gold, which will be pretty much the same no matter where they come from. Commodities that are extracted or mined from the ground are referred to as 'hard' commodities, while those that are farmed or grown on the land are known as 'soft' commodities. Investors typically buy and sell commodities through 'futures'.

Companies House Companies House is where companies are incorporated and dissolved. It provides a register of all the information companies are legally required to supply, making it available to the public for free.

Competition and Markets Authority An independent organization that aims to foster competition by ensuring that consumers have plenty of options. It prevents companies from holding a monopoly on a given industry.

compound interest This is worked out by taking the interest earned for a set period, adding it back to the total, and then calculating the interest for the next period, and so on, which means you are earning interest on interest, as well as the interest earned on the original amount.

consideration The amount paid for something.

Consumer Price Index This is used to measure inflation and deflation. The Consumer Price Index takes the average price of a basket of goods and tracks how much it costs over time. When the cost rises, that's inflation. If the basket becomes cheaper, that's deflation.

contract for difference (CFD) This is a tradable contract between a buyer and his or her broker, betting on the performance of a share, currency, commodity or index over a set period of time.

convertible bond This is a bond with a possible stock option hidden inside. It can be converted from a bond to an equity stake if required.

Corporation Tax The tax levied on a company's profits.

correction A movement of at least 10% in the value of a stock, bond, commodity or index, which corrects an overvaluation – or occasionally an undervaluation. Corrections can occur before recessions and can hint at a bear market to come.

cost of dealing This will include commission, spread (the difference between the buying and selling prices) and stamp duty.

coupon The interest paid on a bond, usually expressed as a percentage. If you have a bond worth £1,000, with a coupon of 7%, it will pay £70 a year or £35 twice a year. Also known as the 'nominal yield' or 'bond yield'.

cover A way to lower exposure to risk. Can refer to a hedging action, in case a market doesn't perform as expected.

credit rating A credit rating is an opinion about a borrower's ability to meet his or her financial commitments. Credit ratings agencies include Standard & Poor's, Moody's and Fitch.

crowdfunding Raising the funds for a business or project from multiple small investors.

current yield The annual income from a bond divided by the present value of that bond. Because it's based on the current market value of the bond, this can be unreliable – prices change. Also called 'dividend yield' for shares. If a bond is priced at £100 and pays out an annual coupon of £5, the current yield is 5%. Actual return depends on the price of the bond when you sell it, which could be higher or lower than £100.

dead cat bounce A temporary rally after a steep decline. The rally is short-lived and followed by another fall – because even a dead cat will bounce if you drop it from a great height.

debenture A type of bond based on pure debt, so it can only be issued by companies that are extremely unlikely to go bust.

debt/equity ratio A ratio showing total debts relative to shareholders' equity. The higher the number, the more likely the company could be adversely affected by rising interest rates or an economic downturn.

default A company defaults when it is unable to pay either the interest on its debt or the outstanding debt itself.

depreciation The decrease in value of an asset over time, as accounted for on the balance sheet.

derivative A financial asset that derives its value from the performance of another asset. The underlying asset is usually stocks, bonds, commodities, currencies or market indices.

dilution When a shareholding decreases in value because new shares have been issued to raise new capital, diluting the overall pool. Investors accept dilution because they believe the fundraising will help that company become more profitable, so they may own a smaller slice but the pie has grown a lot bigger.

discretionary Where a client allows their investment manager to take control of how their portfolio is run, and no approval is required.

dividend These are pay-outs to company shareholders. Dividends are issued when a company is profitable, if the business doesn't need to reinvest all its profit back into growth. Mutual funds and exchange-traded funds also pay out dividends.

dividend cover This shows the ability of a company to maintain current levels of dividend.

dividend yield The dividend paid out per share divided by the market price of the share.

due diligence An audit of a potential investment, which means going through financial records and other material with a fine-tooth comb.

early-stage company A start-up, which usually means the company is younger than five years old. These are typically riskier than more established companies.

earnings The US term for profit.

earnings per share (EPS) This figure takes the total net profit and divides it by the number of shares to determine how much the company actually earned. This is not a reliable number on its own, as companies have been known to manipulate the numbers to show an EPS that suits its purposes. Always look at other financial measures too, such as cash flow.

EBITDA Earnings before interest, tax, depreciation and amortization. This means the profit before all the charges that have nothing to do with operating costs are taken out. This number is often used by companies that are trying to appear more profitable than they are. Profit before tax is seen as a healthier measure.

emerging market This is a bit of a retro phrase given that many of the markets classed as 'emerging' emerged a while back – China, for example. Broadly, it means a country where income per capita is classed as low to middling, where growth is predicted to outpace developed markets, such the UK, the United States and Japan.

Enterprise Investment Scheme (EIS) A UK tax relief created to encourage investors to back early-stage and risky start-ups with up to £1 million.

entrepreneur A business owner.

equities Stocks and shares. Or, in property, the amount that your investment is worth less the mortgage on it.

exchange-traded fund (ETF) These funds track an underlying asset, such as an index, a commodity, a bond or a whole bunch of different things all inside one basket. ETFs are traded on the stock exchange like shares, which means they have more liquidity than mutual funds, and they often come with lower fees, too.

extraordinary general meeting (EGM) A meeting of shareholders and other stakeholders, such as employees, to discuss an issue or change of circumstance at a company. An EGM is called because the problem is too serious or urgent to wait until the official AGM, and the company requires an immediate vote – or help – from shareholders.

fixed-income securities Typically bonds. These are the types of asset that pay out a fixed rate of income. The borrower, or bond issuer, pays a set amount of interest – the coupon – until a certain date, in return for a loan. When the bond reaches maturity, the original amount – the principal – is returned. Because the income is guaranteed, it tends to be lower than other kinds of securities.

forward contract A private agreement to buy or sell something at a specified price at a future date. It's a way of hedging: one party is worried that the price of the asset might rise, the other that it will fall. Imagine that Lucy wants to sell a crop of blackberries at harvest time. Luke wants to buy the fruit, so they agree that he will pay her £5,000. By the time the blackberries are ripe, the market value of the crop might be higher or lower than £5,000, but this is the price they are comfortable to pay. If there's a drought or a blackberry blight, the blackberries might be worth £7,000. Or there might be a glut, meaning they are worth only £3,000. In this scenario, Lucy was shorting the price, while Luke was entering into a long forward contract.

FTSE 100 The UK's top 100 companies. FTSE is short for Financial Times Stock Exchange, also colloquially called the Footsie. The FTSE 100 is made up of the largest firms on the London Stock Exchange, representing around 80% of its total value. It is used as a barometer for the health of the UK economy.

FTSE 250 If the FTSE 100 is the top 100 UK companies, the FTSE 250 is the next 250. Good for gauging the health of smaller companies. The term FTSE 350 is used to describe the combined FTSE 100 and FTSE 250.

fund supermarket A platform offering the choice of a wide array of mutual funds – a one-stop shop. These are also known as 'platforms', 'fund shops', 'fund brokers' or 'investment shops'.

futures Futures are financial contracts whereby a buyer and seller agree on a deal to trade an asset, be it a physical commodity such as wheat, or a financial instrument, at a set date for a predetermined price. Unlike forward contracts, these can be traded on an exchange.

gearing A way of describing how much debt a company is carrying. Gearing weighs debt against the value of the company – its equity. Therefore a highly geared company is one with a lot of debt relative to equity, making it a riskier investment because it may not be able to pay off what it owes. Also called 'leverage'.

gilts Gilts are British government bonds. They are usually considered low-risk investments as the possibility of the government defaulting on its debt is very low. The name 'gilt' was inspired by the design of the original certificates, which had golden – or gilded – edges.

going public See *initial public offering.*

hedge A way to offset risk by betting on one outcome and an opposite outcome simultaneously. The famous is phrase is 'hedge your bets'. Hedges can be 'perfect', which means they have eliminated all risk, or 'imperfect', whereby there may still be losses. Hedges often involve derivatives, such as futures, options, swaps and forward contracts.

hedge fund This is a fund that typically makes high-risk investments to generate big returns. Such funds are called hedge funds because they may use hedging to offset some of the risk, such as shorting futures on a company while still holding the actual stock and hoping it will appreciate. Hedge funds typically make leveraged investments – where they use borrowed money to bet on the market. This can generate much higher returns but is also risky. Retail investors don't tend to get involved with hedge funds – these giants are in bed with institutional investors such as pension funds.

illiquid An asset that is not easy to convert into cash.

index A ranking of securities, such as stocks or bonds. The FTSE 100 is an example of a well-known index.

index tracker A fund that tracks the performance of an index. A FTSE 100 index tracker will invest in all 100 companies, and deliver returns based on the performance of the whole portfolio. Index trackers are a way to invest passively in securities – unlike active investing, which involves a fund manager picking stocks he or she believes will outperform the market.

inflation The measure of how fast the price of goods and services rises over time. In a high-inflation environment, the currency is devalued because it can't buy as many goods. In a deflationary environment, the price of goods and services falls. Inflation is measured using one of two rates, the Consumer Price Index (CPI) or the Retail Price Index (RPI). These are calculated slightly differently, and RPI includes the costs of housing, such as mortgage interest costs and council tax.

initial public offering (IPO) When a private company issues stock to the public for the first time. Also known as going public. Businesses go public in order to raise capital, but being publicly traded brings an extra layer of regulation and public scrutiny.

insolvent If a company – or an individual – is unable to repay its debt, or the interest payments on its debt, it becomes insolvent. An insolvency practitioner may be engaged to help creditors get some of their money back. Not to be confused with bankruptcy, although they essentially mean a similar thing. Insolvency is your financial state, while bankruptcy is the legal state arising from that insolvency; you can file for bankruptcy once you are unable to pay down your debts.

instrument Any asset purchased by an investor is a financial instrument: a metaphorical gold violin on which to play a tune named 'Profit', hopefully. Instruments can be physical assets, such as houses, or they can be equity or debt, such as shares or bonds, respectively.

interest cover A measure of how easily the firm can manage to repay its debt.

investment bank Commercial banks deal with mortgages, savings and current accounts, while investment banks offer specialized services for companies and large investors. These include helping companies to do deals, such as IPOs or mergers, undertaking research and helping customers to manage risk. Investment banks also buy and sell securities in their own right for profit. Many commercial banks have investment banking divisions.

investment grade Bonds or securities that are regarded as unlikely to default. Usually securities with ratings from AAA to BBB.

investment trust An entity quoted on the stock exchange that invests in other companies and securities. Its trade price depends on supply and demand rather than purely on the value of its investments.

junk bond This is a bond that typically carries a high risk of default but a high yield as a result. Junk bonds carry a credit rating of BB or lower from the ratings agency Standard & Poor's, or below Ba from Moody's. Bonds are rated on their ability to pay out the promised income and return the original loan, or principal. Bonds with a high credit rating are known as investment-grade bonds.

leverage A way of using debt to finance an investment. Futures and options are examples of leveraged investments because the same amount of money that would be required to buy 10 shares, say, could be used to control many times that number through an options contract. Think of the way that using a lever acts as a force multiplier – making it easier to open a paint-pot lid, for example. Leverage brings more risk because, while it amplifies gains, it can also exacerbate losses, as the investor can lose more than the initial deposit. Leverage also just means debt. See *gearing*.

liquidity The liquidity of a market represents the ease with which an asset or security can be quickly bought or sold without affecting its price. Cash is the most liquid asset, whereas art or vintage guitars may be much harder to sell, meaning they are illiquid. A seller who wants to offload a painting today may be forced to accept a lower price because there isn't a ready pool of waiting buyers.

London Stock Exchange The UK's primary stock exchange, the LSE is now the largest in Europe. It can trace its history back to 1698.

long Investors take a long position when they expect the value of an asset, such as a share, to rise in value. This is the opposite of a short position, where you expect the security to fall in value. When you own a stock, you take a long position, because you are waiting for your investment to appreciate. This is in contrast to shorting a future, where you don't actually own the stock; instead, you own a financial instrument based on that underlying stock.

management fees Fees charged by investment managers for running portfolios or mutual funds for clients.

margin When you use borrowed money to buy securities. In a more general business context, it means the difference between the cost of buying goods and the selling price, thus determining the profit. See also *profit margin*.

margin call When a broker demands that an investor deposits more money in his or her account to meet minimum capital requirements – also known as the 'minimum maintenance margin'. Margin calls happen when securities bought on margin decrease in value instead of going up, which means they are always greeted with dread.

market capitalization The total value of a publicly traded company's shares. This is the measure used to rank companies on stock exchanges.

market maker An intermediary that facilitates the financial transactions that provide market liquidity. Think of the market maker as the casino and the investor as the gambler – the market maker is always making the opposite bet, and holds enough money to pay out if the gambler wins. Unlike casinos, market makers charge investors for their services, in the form of the bid to ask spread. See *spread*.

maturity The time at which a financial instrument – usually a bond – matures, which means it ceases to exist. This is the point at which the original loan – or principal – must be paid back to the investor.

mini-bond When is a bond not a bond? When it is a mini-bond. These are unsecured loans to companies – often high-risk, early-stage firms. But they pay out an income just like a bond, and return the initial loan amount to the investor at the end of the term, which is typically three to five years. Mini-bonds are not traded on the stock market, so investors are stuck with them until maturity, and they are subject to much looser regulation than regular bonds.

mutual fund A mutual fund is an investment fund, which pools money from many investors to purchase securities, such as shares and bonds. Mutual funds are actively managed by a professional fund manager. The majority are classed as 'open-ended investments' because new shares can be created to meet demand and redeemed when investors want to get their money out.

NASDAQ A US stock exchange and the second largest in the world, second only to the New York Stock Exchange.

New York Stock Exchange (NYSE) The New York Stock Exchange can trace its history back to 1792, making it the oldest stock exchange in the United States. It is headquartered on Wall Street in lower Manhattan, New York. It is the world's largest stock exchange by market capitalization.

nominal yield See *coupon*.

offer price The selling price for a security.

open-ended fund A type of mutual fund that can issue and redeem shares at any time. This is in contrast to a closed-ended fund, which typically issues all the shares it will ever issue when it is first created, meaning that the only way to get out is to trade your shares to another investor. Unit trusts, open-ended investment companies and hedge funds are all types of open-ended funds.

open-ended investment company (OEIC) A type of unit trust where the bid price and offer price are the same.

option An option is a type of financial derivative. It is a contract between two parties that gives the buyer the right to sell a security at a certain time for an agreed price. The buyer doesn't have to sell, however. See also *call option* and *put option*.

passive fund A fund that reproduces the performance of an index by investing in all the securities represented by that index and passively piggybacking its performance.

pension fund A fund that is managed on behalf of a company and its employees to provide pensions when staff retire. Pension funds typically contain a large pool of money and are therefore institutional investors.

performance fee Fund managers earn performance fees when they generate returns for investors. This is often calculated as a percentage of investment profits to incentivize the fund manager to aim for the greatest gains. Hedge funds tend to charge exceptionally high performance fees.

portfolio A collection of investments.

price/earnings ratio A common way of valuing shares. This financial ratio divides the market value of a company by the post-tax profits.

principal The principal is the amount borrowed from an investor, usually through the sale of a bond. This must be repaid at the end of a set term. Principal can also refer to the balance of a standard loan that is yet to be repaid.

profit margin The profit margin is calculated by subtracting net profit from revenue and dividing it again by revenue. The figure is then shown as a percentage. For example, Bob makes a batch of cakes, which he sells for £500. You take the revenue – £500 – minus the amount Bob spent on ingredients and other expenses, which comes to £250. £500 – £250 = £250. £250 / £500 = 0.5, so the profit margin is 50%.

profit warning When a company makes a public announcement that its profits are likely to be lower than forecast.

put option A put option gives an investor the right, but not the obligation, to sell a stock, bond, commodity or other instrument at an agreed price within a specific time frame. Used in options trading, put options are used when the seller wants or expects the value of the security to fall, so he or she has been paid more money than the asset is worth at a later time.

quarter A period of three months.

redemption When securities are sold back to the issuer in return for cash.

retail investor A private investor making investments on a personal basis, rather than on behalf of a company or organization. Also called a small investor or individual investor.

Retail Price Index (RPI) This is the most commonly used measure of inflation. The Retail Price Index is an index of the current prices of a representative 'basket' of goods. See also *inflation*.

rights issue When a company issues extra shares to raise funds from existing shareholders.

securities Instruments representing financial value, such as bonds or shares.

Seed Enterprise Investment Scheme (SEIS) A UK tax relief created to encourage investors to back early-stage and risky start-ups. The SEIS is for smaller investments of up to £100,000 while the Enterprise Investment Scheme is for up to £1 million.

Self-Invested Personal Pension (Sipp) A do-it-yourself pension. Individuals with a Sipp can make their own investment decisions, and pick from a range of options approved by HMRC to try to build up their pension pot.

share A small piece of a company, also known as a stock. The owner of a share – a shareholder – is entitled to a proportional amount of any profits that are handed out as dividends. You can own shares in entities beyond just companies, such as property and mutual funds.

share price The price at which a single share can be bought or sold.

short This is a way to profit from a decline in value of a company. A short sale refers to the practice of selling borrowed shares with a view to repurchasing them in future – also known as 'covering' – when the price has fallen, and pocketing the difference. This is the opposite of taking a long position. A short seller will make money if the stock goes down in price, while a long position makes money when the stock goes up. If the short sale goes against you, and the shares rise in value, there's no limit to the amount of money you can lose.

solvent A financial term that means a company's assets are greater than its liabilities.

spread There are lots of different kinds of spread, but they all generally refer to the difference between the price to buy an asset and the price to sell it. In currency trading, the spread is the difference between what the broker pays for the currency and the price at which you buy it from the broker, like a commission. In spread betting, it's the difference between the bid and the offer. In equities trading, the spread is the difference between the bid and the ask.

spread betting This is classed as a type of gambling in the UK. Spread betting involves taking a bet on the price movement of a security. There is a bid price and an offer price – the spread – and the investor will decide whether the value of the underlying stock will be higher or lower than the spread. Losses can exceed deposits.

stamp duty A tax that is payable on property and other securities.

stock market (or exchange) The place where shares in publicly traded companies are traded. Stock markets allow companies to trade a small slice of ownership for growth capital.

stop-loss order These are designed to limit the losses that investors can make on their bets on market movements. The stop-loss order is an agreement that the broker will buy or sell a security when it reaches a certain price.

structured product A complex investment that generates returns based on the performance of underlying assets. Unlike tracker funds, which simply want an index, such as the FTSE 100, to go up in value, these products may have more complex rules, and can result in investors losing more than their initial deposit. Structured products have been embroiled in their fair share of financial scandals. See also *derivative*.

trading floor The place where traders buy and sell assets in exchanges, investment banks and brokerages. Known as 'the pit' and often portrayed in films as bustling areas with hundreds of traders in coloured waistcoats screaming into telephones, but, these days, often just the physical location of the trading division, where deals are done quietly through computers.

underlying asset The asset that a derivative product is basing its price on, such as a share or commodity or futures. Think of the derivative as riding on the coat-tails of the underlying asset.

underlying share The share that a derivative product is based upon, often futures and options. See *underlying asset*.

unit trust A type of mutual fund that will hold assets and pay profits out to the owners of the fund – or unit owners. A unit trust is an example of an open-ended fund, as it creates more units to accommodate new investors, and allows units to be redeemed to make the fund smaller if demand falls.

utilities A sector made up of the privatized gas, electricity and water industries.

value investing A style of investing popularized by Benjamin Graham, author of *The Intelligent Investor*, which involves buying stocks that are trading at a discount to their actual value. Rather than simply looking for bargains, superstar investor Warren Buffet has said that it's about 'finding an outstanding company at a sensible price'.

venture capital fund Investment funds that specialize in backing early-stage to mid-size companies with strong growth potential. These investments are classed as high risk with potentially high returns.

venture capital trust Entities that make venture capital investments, offering investors the opportunity to benefit from the tax advantages of doing so.

warrant A tradable security that gives the holder the right to purchase a specific number of shares at a specified date in the future.

yield The return that an investor will make – typically in a year – from an investment, through either interest or dividend payments. This figure is often expressed as a percentage of the value of the investment. There are lots of different kinds of yield. See *current yield*, *coupon* and *yield to maturity*.

yield to maturity This is the total return from a bond, presuming that it is held until maturity. The calculation is complex, but assumes that all coupon payments are reinvested and gives an annualized rate of return for the life of the bond. Yield to maturity is also known as 'redemption yield' or 'book yield'.

INDEX

Note: page numbers in *italic* indicate figures.

Also available from **Kogan Page**

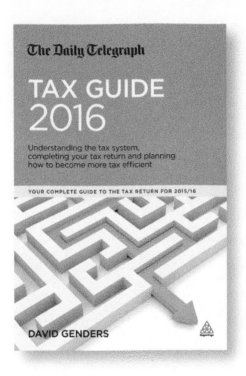

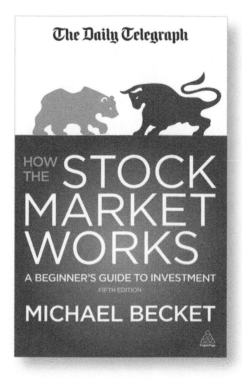